TEA

BILL

This book is the first to treat Billiards and Snooker with any degree of comprehensiveness in a single volume, and I sincerely hope it may be the means of helping the vast number of ambitious young players who wish to play well to gain a practical understanding of the technique and strategy of Billiards and Snooker; games, which, as I have sought to stress, are complementary and interrelated.

The Author

... outstanding in that it treats billiards and snooker comprehensively in a single volume ... will undoubtedly take its place as a standard work among text books on the two popular games with which it deals.

Sports Teacher

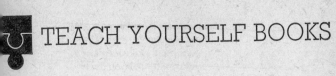

TEACH YOURSELF BOOKS

BILLIARDS AND SNOOKER

Richard Holt

Editor of *Billiards and Snooker*
formerly *The Billiard Player*

ST. PAUL'S HOUSE WARWICK LANE LONDON EC4P 4AH

First printed 1957
Sixth impression (with corrections) 1969
Tenth impression 1973

ISBN 0 340 05523 5

Printed and bound in England
for The English Universities Press Ltd
by Hazell Watson & Viney Ltd, Aylesbury

FOREWORD

Billiards and Snooker are games which call for intensified practice from an early age if the maximum standard is to be achieved, for they require an almost automatic degree of precision in striking and control. For obvious reasons, amateurs are not in a position to make the game a life's calling as are professionals. Nevertheless, there are thousands of youths and young men, such is the widespread popularity of these games, whose earnest wish it is to improve and reach a reasonable standard of mastery in them.

This volume is the first to treat Billiards *and* Snooker with any degree of comprehensiveness in a single volume, and I sincerely hope it may be the means of helping the vast number of ambitious young players who wish to play well to gain a practical understanding of the technique and strategy of Billiards and Snooker; games, which, as I have sought to stress, are complementary and interrelated. There are also, besides these young enthusiasts, vast numbers—for it is estimated that from four to five million play the games in one form or another, that is, seriously or for recreative purposes—of middle-aged and even elderly people who would like to know more about the art of the game. I hope that they too may derive both profit and pleasure from the book. I particularly stress the fact that even if the reader be interested in, or concerned with, only one of the two games, he should not omit to read and study the section dealing with the other, as they are based on the same cue technique.

In these pages I have tried to offer a substantial fund of practical knowledge and instruction, and I believe the book covers all the ground needful to know what to do and how to do it. I feel sure, moreover, that the young player who absorbs its contents and practises hard will find that he will attain a high degree of skill and be equipped to shine in the highest amateur circles.

All that is needed is industry, perseverance and enthusiasm, and old Samuel Smiles' gospel of self-help, as potent a means as ever when it comes to fulfilling legitimate ambition, will, as it has always done, bring success.

RICHARD HOLT

NOTE (1964 Impression)

Every reader is advised to procure a copy of the official Rules of both games. Those of each game may be had separately, and the official *Handbook and Rules* contains the rules of both games amongst its varied contents. It is not permissible to include the Rules in this volume as they are copyright, and are an important source of the official body's income. Many of the Rules have been quoted, but, for the reason stated, complete inclusion is not possible. Every serious player should thoroughly understand the rules of the game he is playing, and many a player has suffered by lack of such knowledge.

NOTE (1969 Impression)

Since 1964 a few changes have occurred in the rules of Billiards and Snooker. As previously stressed, every serious player should study the rules thoroughly. A copy of the Rules can be obtained from the Billiards Association and Control Council, 15, Exeter Street, Strand, London, W.C.2. This body also publishes a monthly journal, *Billiards and Snooker* which deals with every aspect of the games, including rule changes, technical articles, championship information, etc., etc. The official *Handbook and Rules* also contains full records of the game.

The most important rule change, made on September 1st, 1968, concerns Billiards. During 1964, the fact that Snooker was more extensively played than Billiards induced the Billiards Association to make a change in the rules, whereby

the pot or winning hazard, which, of course, is the basic
stroke in snooker, might be given more scope in the three-ball
game, thus encouraging snooker players to take up billiards
and maybe enter the Billiards Championship.

Accordingly, the rule which required the red ball to be
placed on the Centre Spot after being twice pocketed in
succession off the Billiard Spot was altered to read: "When the
red ball is pocketed it shall always be replaced on the Billiard
Spot". Winning or Losing Hazards (i.e. pots or in-offs) were,
at the time, limited to 15 in succession. So that, in conjunction
with the new rule change, it was now possible for a player to
pot the red ball off the Billiard Spot 15 times consecutively.
This innovation, however, although seemingly popular for
some time, gradually caused the monotony of repetition, as
billiards threatened to become, like snooker, a game in which
potting predominated. A change, therefore, became imperative
and on September 1st, 1968, a new rule was introduced. This
reduced the number of pots which could be made with the red
ball off its Spot to 5, after which the red had to be placed on
the Centre Spot. The limitation of hazards to 15 was, however,
retained so that, if a player makes his 5 pots off the Spot and
manages to keep going for 15 pots, he then has to make a
cannon to continue his break. It is, of course, still possible for
a player to play the strict top-of-the-table game, with 4
possible pots in succession instead of the mere one allowed by
the top-end game (see pages 104 to 122) before transferring
the red to the Centre Spot, but the attractive interplay of pot
and cannon would be necessarily limited, for, with 4 pots
possible before transferring to the Centre Spot, the potting
element would greatly predominate. At the time of writing, it
will be necessary to wait and see how the new (1968) rule
works out before judging its merits.

CONTENTS

N.B.—(S) means that this section applies to Snooker also.

PLEASE NOTE

In all diagrams a straight line ———— represents the path of the cue-ball and a broken one - - - - - - that of the object-balls. A dot-and-dash line ·-·-·-·-·- has been used in some instances to avoid confusion in a diagram containing a number of strokes. An arrow generally denotes the direction, not necessarily the stopping-place, of the cue- or object-ball.

To save space the following abbreviations have been used throughout the book. The terms are, however, printed in full when first mentioned. The reader is recommended to write them out on a slip of paper, thus obviating the necessity for continually referring back to this page.

Half ball	= h-b
Quarter-ball	= $\frac{1}{4}$-b
Three-quarter ball	= $\frac{3}{4}$-b
Cue-ball	= c-b
Object-ball	= o-b
Right-hand	= r-h
Left-hand	= l-h
Bottom pocket(s)	= bot-pkt(s)
Top pocket(s)	= top-pkt(s)
Middle pocket(s)	= mid-pkt(s)
Diagram(s)	= D; Ds.
Drop cannon	= d-c

Here and there throughout the book, repetition has been made of important technical features on the principle that a thing twice said is more easily remembered.

"Side" is treated on pages 41 to 51, but allusions to it necessarily occur previous to that section. It will be well, therefore, to give the reader a definition of the various types of Side in advance: Side consists of hitting the c-b on either of its sides, i.e. off centre, to promote a lateral "throw-off". "Running" Side increases the angle of the throw-off; "check"

Side decreases it. Either of these types may be r-h or l-h Side. "Pocket" Side is that which assists the entry of the c-b into a pocket off the jaw of the latter.

"Plain ball" striking means striking the c-b exactly at its centre, that is, without Side.

R-h Side may be "running" or "check", or "pocket" Side, the same with l-h Side. To help the reader, in most cases the fact of its being "running" or "check" or "pocket" Side has been added to the type of Side, i.e. right-hand or left-hand.

"Top" means striking the c-b above centre; "Bottom", below its centre.

The angle of incidence is the angle at which a ball contacts a cushion; the angle of reflection is the angle at which it leaves it. In theory, these angles are equal in plain-ball strokes (i.e. without Side); in practice, not always so; degrees of force, for instance, altering them. In general, however, they form a reliable working basis.

BILLIARDS

INTRODUCTORY

Billiards is a game which demands the utmost precision of eye and touch, and the nearer the physical action involved approaches the mechanical, the more successful will be the mastery achieved. The person who desires to become a first-class Billiard player, or even a capable one, is faced at the outset, as he is in other games, with the task of mastering the basic principles; in short, he must learn to walk before he tries to run. Now the majority of those essaying the game do the contrary. They have seen Billiards played and, liking it, take a cue in hand at the first opportunity and proceed to knock the balls about in the way they have seen others do, and, without paying the slightest heed to first principles, develop a more or less haphazard style of play which leads nowhere. This fact accounts for the mediocrity of thousands of players in clubs, halls and the like, and explains why many of our modern young men come to the conclusion that Billiards is too difficult, and take to Snooker instead.

What is the mistake they make? Simply this. They have not realized that the art of Billiards depends on certain preliminary essentials: stance, the bridge, true, that is, straight cueing; and that when these have been definitely determined, after due experiment, the theory of the game itself must be studied along with the technique of execution. Failure to do these things explains, as I have said above, the multiplicity of inferior players, and, conversely, due attention to them results in varying degrees of mastery. It also involves, what the mastery of all arts and games involves, hard work.

In the present work I have sought to initiate the player into the first principles and general technique of Billiards and Snooker; in a word, to place the theory of these games before him, and he can rest assured that if he is prepared to practise enthusiastically on the lines laid down he cannot but become a very good player, and if he possesses a special aptitude for either game, perhaps one of champion class.

I would at the outset impress upon the reader that the most vital element in Billiards and Snooker is *true cueing*, that is, the correct manipulation of the cue and making of the stroke. All the knowledge in the world will not bring mastery if the player's cueing is faulty. Billiards and Snooker depend on accuracy of ball contacts, and these, in their turn, derive from holding and wielding the cue in perfect accordance with the line of aim.

Therefore, I strongly advise the student not to minimize this fundamental part of Billiards and Snooker technique, and, having adopted some sort of ready-made stance and delivery, to take it for granted that he has mastered the preliminaries for good, and need not bother any more about them. On the contrary, he must be permanently mindful of them and, by always keeping an eye on his cueing, and testing it by one-ball practice, ensure that no bad habits have crept in.

IMPLEMENTS OF THE GAME

I take it for granted that all readers know that Billiards is played on a large table with a slate bed, the surface of which is covered with a woollen cloth, green in colour, and that the game itself consists of scoring points by striking one of three balls with a wooden cue to contact the other two, or one of the two.

Let us now examine the implements used:

The Table: A slate bed, inset in a wooden framework and covered by a green woollen cloth, tautly drawn and having a nap running from one end to the other, forms the playing area. The table measures 12 ft. by 6 ft. $1\frac{1}{2}$ in., but the bed, being enclosed by rubber cushions which overhang it by 2 in., is reduced for playing purposes to an area of 11 ft. 8 in. by 5 ft. $9\frac{1}{2}$ in. The table rests on eight legs, and at each corner is a network pocket and one at each (long) side, exactly in the

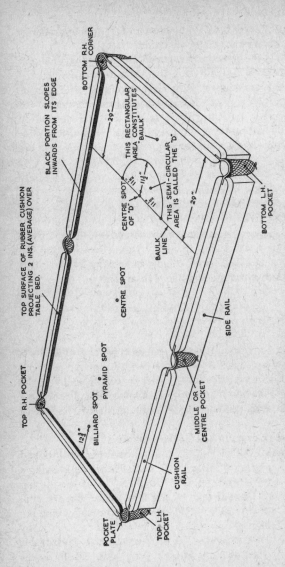

CONSTITUENTS OF TABLE SURFACE, CUSHIONS, ETC., SHOWING TABLE MARKINGS.

D.1

middle, making six in all. The slate bed is cut away at each
pocket position, likewise the rubber cushion, to permit the balls
to enter. The pocket openings must conform to the templets
of the Billiards Association and Control Council. The four
corner pockets have a width of $3\frac{1}{2}$ in. across the spot where the
fall of the slate commences (and $3\frac{3}{8}$ in. from tip to tip of the
templets), but pockets are made to fit the templets and
measurements are not given in the official Rules. The middle
pockets are, approximately, 4 in. across, at the fall of the
slate. The height of the table, from the floor to the top of the
woodwork rail, must measure from 2 ft. $9\frac{1}{2}$ in. to 2 ft. $10\frac{1}{2}$ in.
The rail adjoins the rubber projection or overhang referred to,
and on its outer side is of wood, as stated.

The Markings of the Table: A line drawn 29 in. from the
face (or projection) of the bottom cushion, and parallel with it,
is called the "Baulk-line", and the area within this and the
bottom cushion is called "Baulk". From the centre of this line
a semi-circle on the "Baulk" or inner side of the line is
marked, with a radius of $11\frac{1}{2}$ in.; it encloses an area which is
called the "D". There are four spots marked on the table,
by means of minute wafer-like pieces of silk. These are
situated: (1) at the centre of the "D"; (2) at the centre of the
table (i.e. the playing area), it is called the *Centre Spot*;
(3) at a point $12\frac{3}{4}$ in. from the face of the "top" cushion, the
Billiard Spot; and (4) at a point half-way between the Centre
Spot and the face of the top cushion, this is called the *Pyramid
Spot*. The four spots are situated on an imaginary central-
longitudinal line of the table. There are also two other spots,
one at each end of the "D" line, but only the r-h one is used
in Billiards (see Rule 8). Both, however, are used in
Snooker. The "bottom" end of the table is that containing the
Baulk area; the "top" end is, of course, the other end. To play
up the table is to play facing the top; to play down the table
is to play facing the bottom. "Below" the middle pockets is
the half of the table containing the Baulk; "above" the middle
pockets refers to the half containing the Pyramid and Billiard
Spots.

The Cue: This is a long wooden "stick" (invariably of ash or maple), which must not be less than 3 ft. and is generally about 4 ft. 10 in. long, and gradually tapers from a thickish butt, about 1 in. in diameter, to a thin end or rounded top, to which a leather tip is fixed either by a wafer or by glue. This tip is 11 millimetres in width, though such width varies. The tip surface being shiny, a piece of special chalk is used to roughen it after each two or three strokes, to prevent it from sliding off the cue-ball. The balance of the cue is achieved by weighting the butt.

The Balls: Three balls, made from compositions called crystalate, bonzoline, etc., are used, two being white and the other red. They must be equal in size and weight, and should be of a diameter of $2\frac{1}{16}$ to $2\frac{3}{32}$ in. Ivory balls, from elephant tusks, were formerly used but were officially discarded about 1930 and have become obsolete. Crystalate balls are almost exclusively used nowadays.

THE PLAN OF THE GAME

The white ball which the player strikes with his cue is called the "cue-ball"; the other two (one white, one red) are called the "object-balls". Each player uses one of the white balls, which are distinguished from each other by one, called "Spot", being marked with a black spot at opposite extremities. The other is called "Plain". The players toss or "string" for choice of balls, the winner declaring, "I'll take Plain" or "I'll take Spot".

To "String".—This means that each player directs, with his cue, from "hand" (i.e. from the Baulk-line) a white ball "up the table", that is, to the top cushion, and the player who succeeds in causing his ball to come to rest nearer the bottom cushion, whether it rebounds or not, is the winner, and has choice of balls, and of playing first or second, as he wishes. Preference for Spot or Plain is mainly an idiosyncratic choice as, of course, each ball exactly resembles the other, but it happens that some players prefer the one or the other. The winner of the toss or "stringing" thus has choice of balls, and of "breaking" (commencing the game) or asking his opponent to "break". The strategy of the start of the game will be explained later.

Scoring: The player who scores most points wins. Scoring is achieved as follows:

1. *By Cannons.*—A cannon is made by causing the c-b (i.e. the ball propelled by the player's cue) to contact the two o-b's in succession. Two points are scored by a cannon, whether it be from white to red, or red to white.

2. *By "Losing Hazards"* (*"Losers"*).—A losing hazard is made by causing the c-b to enter a pocket after contact with one of the two o-b's. A losing hazard off the red is rewarded by 3 points; off the white, by 2.

3. *By "Winning Hazards"* (*or "Pots"*).—A winning hazard, or pot, is made by making the c-b contact one or other of the two o-b's, and causing it (the o-b) to enter a pocket. "Potting", or pocketing, the red ball scores 3 points; potting the white, 2. Potting the white (i.e. the opponent's ball) is done for defensive purposes only, as I will explain later.

It is possible to make a cannon in conjunction with a losing or winning hazard, although it is only exceptionally that such a stroke is played for. Any stroke which is not played for scores, but is called a "fluke", and by a fluke (the stroke is never played for) it is possible to pocket all three balls, a 10-stroke, but this does not enter into serious Billiards, and is, as stated, an egregious fluke. Flukes are frequent when hard-hitting or haphazard players are "performing", or mere novices: good players, of course, get flukes only very occasionally. Nevertheless, flukes count at Billiards as they do at other games, and the player continues at the table. Very big "breaks" have been made after a fluked stroke at the start.

When a losing hazard and cannon are made in the same stroke, the player scores two points for the cannon and two for the hazard, if the white be struck first, and two for the cannon and three for the hazard, if red be struck first. If both object-balls are struck simultaneously, and a hazard is made as well, two points are scored for the cannon, and two for the hazard. If more than one hazard, or a combination of hazards and cannons are made in the same stroke, all are scored.

A "Break".—While the player continues to score he remains at the table, and only after missing a stroke does his visit or "turn" end, whereupon his opponent takes his place. To score a number of points, by a sequence of successful strokes, whether the total be 10, 20, 50, 100 or more (theoretically, he might carry on to the end of the game by never missing!), is to make a "break". The record break, by orthodox Billiards, that is, excluding specialized shots which were subsequently barred or restricted, is 4,137, by Walter Lindrum of Australia (1932).

The purpose of the game is, as implied above, to make, in sequence, as many cannons, losing and winning hazards as possible, and thereby to score more points than one's opponent. The *art* of the game, however, is so to contrive that one successful stroke leaves, when the balls have come to rest, another opportunity of scoring; in other words, by control of the balls to leave one scoring opportunity after another. To put it another way: to make an ordered sequence of scoring strokes by aiming each time, not only to score, but also to leave the balls *in perfect position* for the next stroke. The indifferent player concentrates on the actual success of the stroke, leaving "position" more or less to chance; the true Billiard player, that is, the skilled artist, takes, in a way, the stroke's success for granted, giving priority to after-position. The average player makes a good break only occasionally, and even after playing for years may not have made a true (i.e. purposefully made) break of over 30 or 40; the good amateur and student of the game consistently makes good breaks, and is ever improving by cultivation of the art of touch or strength (that is, striking the balls with varying degrees of force, from soft or gentle to strong or forceful, as the stroke, both from the scoring and positional standpoints, demands). In a word, good Billiards is the art of controlling the balls and working them in harmonious or skilfully gauged fashion.

STANCE, DELIVERY, CUEING

As I have said, the paucity of first-rate amateur Billiard players amongst the countless numbers who play the game is due to neglect of first principles, and, amongst the latter, the way to stand, to make a bridge and how to address and strike the ball take the first place, for, although a player's ideas on the subject of policy, that is, what to do with the balls, may be quite wrong, they can be rectified up to a comparatively advanced stage of his career, but once a bad style of cueing or an awkward stance is developed, it is supremely difficult, if not impossible, to alter it.

It is, therefore, of paramount importance to settle these things in the right way at the very start, otherwise trouble lies ahead, for, from ingrained habit, even though he may try hard to eradicate faults of stance and cueing, he will find himself reverting automatically to the old ways. It is not possible to lay down hard-and-fast rules for the stance, for every player's physique, of course, is, in its way, unique, and what is suitable for a short player is entirely unsuitable for a tall one. It is useful in this respect to take a look at a skilled player who is built more or less on the same lines as oneself, and to "try out" his stance, assuming it itself is orthodox. In any case, the "actions" of various first-class players should be carefully studied, both from a side view and a rear.

Stance

Lay the left forearm on the table, thus anchoring the required position of the body. Plant both feet firmly, with the left leg well forward, knee slightly bent (it is this leg which supports the weight of the body), and the left foot pointing somewhat to the right of the cue line (D.2).

The right leg, comfortably distant, forms the fulcrum or

support of the stance, and the right foot should rest at 2 or 3 in. less than a right angle to the left.

The player, however, must be careful not to cramp his freedom of movement by a too-rigid pose of the body, and the stance he ultimately adopts must allow him to feel physically and mentally free to move easily. When he first tries to fashion his stance, which, of course, must ultimately become, so to speak, second nature to him, he should be doing so in relation to a ball (the c-b) intended to be sent straight up the table. Later on, he will find that certain strokes demand a modification of his stance, but, once he has acquired a satisfactory stance, such modifications will follow automatically. The firmness of the stance *should not be relaxed until the stroke is completed*.

Arm Action

In striking the ball, the only part of the body which moves is the cueing arm, of which the forearm furnishes the main motive power, the upper part of the arm also, and necessarily, moving slightly. The main movement is, as stated, made by the forearm. To a person sitting behind the player, the latter's arm should, from the ideal point of view, move like a piston rod, and in an absolutely straight path, or line. The nearer the player can get to this machine-like movement and alignment, the better will be his execution. The majority of players, even many first-class ones, evince, for physical reasons, a lateral tendency of the arm, and the elbow projects outwards. It is, however, obvious that the farther the arm strays from alignment with the cue, the more difficult it is to aim straight. In model cueing the thumb of the right hand should lightly brush against the player's side, and this fact acts as a reliable guide to the learner in the matter of cue alignment.

The Bridge

I have said that the left forearm should be laid flat on the table. If the player does this, and then lays also his hand flat as well, he is in a position to make his bridge. This he can do by drawing up his fingers and hand ball-wise, until the knuckles have reached their uttermost height consistent with the wrist and finger-tips still resting firmly on the table. The thumb should now be raised, with its main or lower joint adhering firmly to the "body" of the hand. The tip-end of the cue should now be placed between the thumb and first finger. The thumb tip should project outwards as much as is comfortably practicable. Instead, however, of keeping to what may feel like a rigid or cramped position, the hand may be relaxed somewhat, so that the position and bridge causes no strain. Keep sliding the cue backwards and forwards, until the movement is easy and unimpeded. It is not necessary to keep the thumb unduly high. So long as the bridge permits a flowing slide of the cue, and the thumb prevents it wobbling or moving laterally, the bridge will function accurately. The fingers, it is important to add, should maintain a fairly firm grip of the cloth, for, if they are loose, the bridge will be loose, which would make true cueing impossible. To test your stance, etc., ask a friend to verify how near the following you are to being on a straight line: Front view: tip of elbow (when drawn back); point of chin; tip-end of cue; c-b (struck at its centre). Back view: toe-cap of shoe; butt-end of cue; elbow joint; cue-tip, c-b (when struck at its centre). Deviation may occur with some players at this point or that, but the coincidence of such elements is the "ideal", and, provided the player's stance conforms approximately to these specifications, there will not be much, if anything, wrong with his stance.

HERBERT BEETHAM (DERBY), three times winner of the English Amateur Billiards Championship. The photo illustrates Beetham's perfect cueing technique.

Holding of the Cue

The main thing in holding the cue is to feel complete mastery and control of it in relation to the object to be achieved, namely, making the strokes of the game. As these differ, however, it follows that often the cue-hold must be varied. Nevertheless, as in other matters, there is a main principle, and once it is mastered, adaptation to circumstances in which it must be departed from or modified is easy.

Some players favour a light hold, others a firm, incisive one. The former do not excel in strokes requiring force, the latter in phases of the game which call for delicacy. Some players hold the cue in a loop formed by the thumb and one, two or three fingers, and some use all the fingers. Others even clench the hand as a whole as though clasping a person's wrist, which, theoretically, is quite wrong. In general, a light hold is much superior to a tight one. Good players who offend against the first principles of "delivery" technique often point to their achievements, when remonstrated with, as did Edward Diggle, a famous professional of forty years ago, but they lay themselves open to the retort that if they adhered faithfully to such principles their achievements would be even more impressive, though this again may be disputed.

In general the best hold is with the thumb and four

FRANK EDWARDS (STOURBRIDGE), five times winner of the English Amateur Billiards Championship, and runner-up World Amateur Billiards Championship, 1951. Photo depicts the stance and cue delivery of this great player.

fingers, with the grip or pressure centred in thumb and the first two fingers, with just a light touch by the last two. It is, however, essential that there be no stiff or rigid grip. In fact, the less rigid the grip the better, and to bring the palm of the hand into the matter is to put up the "road closed" sign from the very start so far as ultimate mastery is concerned.

The point at which the cue-hold should be made depends on the player's physique. It also depends on what length cue he uses. About 6, 7 or 8 in. from the butt-end (to the middle of the hand) can serve as a normal guide, which the player may adopt as a starting-point for discovering what is best for his particular style of play. As to the distance between his bridge and the cue-tip, this again cannot be categorically fixed. Six to 8 in., however, is a rough guide, and here again the player can gauge his own requirements accordingly.

Cue Movement(s)

I will use the word "slide" for the "backward-and-forward" motion of the cue; the term generally, and, I think, mistakenly, employed is "swing", but swing implies a deviation from horizontality; slide conveys more accurately the straight motion desirable.

The number of times the cue should execute the "to-and-fro" motion is entirely a matter for the individual. The margin of error in losing hazards is greater than in potting, which demands rather more precision, although it is a delusion to assert that potting a ball can be done by contacting it on one point only, for the pocket opening is obviously wider than the width of the ball. Nevertheless, a losing hazard admits of slightly greater departure from perfect accuracy of contact than does a pot; hence the greater the need for pinpoint precision of contact in potting. Perfect accuracy, however, should always be the aim.

Therefore, the necessary aiming process will, except with "first-time" players, that is, those who sight the ball and strike immediately (these are very rare birds!), need more care and deliberation. Snooker players, therefore (for Snooker is based on the pot exclusively), generally make more motions than Billiard players. In Billiards, *the fewer number of movements backwards and forwards the better*, and, having decided where to strike the c-b, the preliminary "addressing" of the ball or placing of the cue-tip near it (anything from $\frac{1}{2}$ in. to less) may be followed, after the backward motion, by the actual striking (forward) motion, but, as I say, if the player feels three, four or more movements assists his accuracy, there is nothing to be said against it. The top-rank professionals (Snooker) often indulge in even fourteen or fifteen motions when potting, for a frame may be lost by missing a pot, but we are dealing with Billiards here. My own method is: place the cue on the bridge, slide it forward to within $\frac{1}{2}$ in. of the c-b, then half distance backward motion, very short forward and backward motion, then the actual striking. This is, I think, the golden mean between first-time striking and a surplus of motions. When placing the cue on the bridge, one may make, of course, a little adjusting movement.

THEORY OF BALL CONTACTS AND AIMS

Having learned to stand properly at the table and how to hold and strike with the cue, let us now study the basic ball contacts, which are: full-ball, half-ball, three-quarter-ball and quarter-ball. By implanting these firmly in our minds, we are enabled to make intermediate contacts when required. To make such contacts is, with the obvious exception of full-ball, called "dividing" the o-b.

As one cannot represent thickness on paper, we must, for the purpose of illustration, imagine the balls to be flat objects, as coins. To achieve h-b contact (the "key" contact, as it were) we aim, through the centre of the c-b at the (central) outside edge of the o-b, thus covering (theoretically) half the o-b with the c-b. Now turn to D.3 (p. 16).

(*Note.*—Ball 1 represents the c-b and o-b in full-ball contact; balls 2, 3 and 4, the c-b contacting the o-b (ball 1) in $\frac{3}{4}$-b, h-b and $\frac{1}{4}$-b contacts.)

To make full-ball aim, we, of course, aim through the centre of the c-b at the centre of the o-b, ball 1 representing both at the moment of contact.

To make h-b contact, we aim, as stated, through the centre of the c-b (not shown) at the outside (central) edge of the o-b (point *B*, ball 1) and *A* will be the point at which the rim of the c-b (theoretically, of course) would intersect the o-b; to achieve $\frac{3}{4}$-b contact, we must clearly aim at a point midway between the points of contact for full- and h-b contacts, namely, *A* and *B* respectively, i.e. at *C* (ball 1), the c-b, in this case, inter-secting the o-b at point *E*, the o-b (ball 1) then being three parts covered (again, theoretically). Now to get $\frac{1}{4}$-b contact, it is clear that we must aim at a point midway between h-b and full-ball contacts, i.e. *A* and *B*, but, of course, *outside* the o-b, namely, *D*, the c-b rim then intersecting the o-b at *C*, thus covering a quarter of its surface. Remember, aim is always through the centre of the c-b.

With these basic contacts firmly established in our minds, we

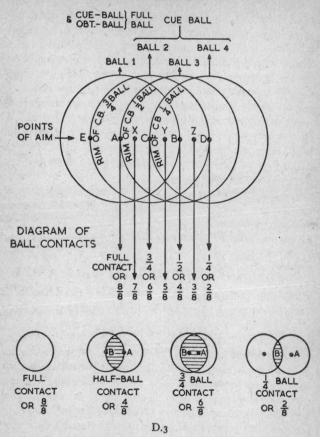

DIAGRAM OF
BALL CONTACTS

D.3

can easily determine the intermediate ones. If we call the full contact, eight-eighths; the h-b, four-eighths; ¾-b, six-eighths; and a ¼-b, two-eighths, we shall see that the intermediate ones will be: seven-eighths, five-eighths and three-eighths, as shown by the diagram (D.3). The latter shows that the points of contact in such aims will be X, Y and Z respectively. Nevertheless, such contacts, in numerical parlance, are rather far fetched, and for practical purposes we are accustomed to name these contacts as follows: seven-eighths, a thickish $\frac{3}{4}$-b; five-eighths, a thickish h-b; and three-eighths, a rather thicker than $\frac{1}{4}$-b contact. Nevertheless, the diagram will help the player to gain a precise idea of these intermediate contacts and, by mentally photographing, as it were, the points X, Y and Z (seven-eighths, five-eighths and three-eighths respectively) in relation to the fundamental contacts, C, B and D ($\frac{3}{4}$, h-b and $\frac{1}{4}$-b) he will acquire facility in determining his points of contact, and, as he acquires experience, will become accustomed to adjusting mentally the variations of the four principal contacts.

Actually, of course, balls, being round and not flat, as treated here, cannot merge one into the other. The theory, however, that they can do so coincides perfectly with what happens in actuality and serves ideally for practical play.

IMPORTANCE OF THE HALF-BALL ANGLE AND IN-OFF; BASIC "LOSING HAZARDS"; THE "LONG LOSER" AND THICK RUN-THROUGH LOSER

This h-b angle is in a way the keystone of Billiards, for not only is it the basis of many of the most important strokes but also it enters into a great many others, in which the actual contacts are calculated from the h-b angle. It is easy to see why the h-b, or, as it is also called, the "natural" angle, is selected for priority, for aiming, as we do, through the centre of the c-b at the edge of the o-b we have a specific target, and, as the h-b contact must always produce the same angle of deflection of the c-b, it follows that we have only to spot the c-b in such a way that that line of deflection coincides with our objective, whether it be a pocket or a ball. D.4: A represents the c-b; C, the o-b; and B, the c-b again, as it contacts the o-b. Aiming, through the centre of the c-b, X, at Y, the edge of the o-b, the c-b, after contact, proceeds along the line B to B_1 (angle of reflection), so that the angle B_1—B—D represents the h-b c-b deviation, roughly 33 degrees (33°). As is obvious, although we aim at Y, the c-b contacts the o-b at W, that is, the points of aim and contact differ, as we shall see when dealing with "Potting". The o-b is thrown off at an angle of about 30 degrees, as shown by the lines D—B and B—E (angle D—B—E). A line passing through the centres of the c-b and o-b, at the moment

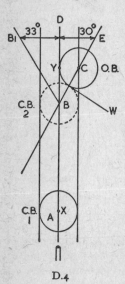

D.4

of impact, here B—C, always indicates the angle of the o-b's throw-off in the h-b stroke (and, of course, in any other stroke). The player's eye, by experience, soon learns to estimate the h-b angle, and the angle at which the o-b is driven should also be committed to ocular memory, for there is, as we shall see, such a thing as the "h-b pot" (represented here by the line B—C—E) and for cannon play also it is invaluable to know what course the o-b will take in such strokes.

D.5 shows a h-b loser into the middle pocket, and once we have learned this angle we are able to adjust our contact for losing hazards which require other than h-b contact (see D.3). If you place the red at a spot 24 in. from the side cushion and 27 in. from the Baulkline, and place the c-b about 4¾ in. to the right of the Centre Spot of the "D" (D.5), you will have a perfect h-b stroke. This stroke you should practise continuously, and I advise you to commit to memory the course taken by the o-b (the red). Of course, this position is only one of a great many from which the h-b loser is practicable into a mid-pkt from the "D".

D.6 shows the basic or "key" h-b losing hazards, and supposing the c-b to be positioned on any part of these lines, the h-b stroke is "on" (i.e. practicable). In strokes 1, 2 and 5 we are playing from the "D" and whenever we play from hand (i.e. the "D") we may place our ball anywhere in the "D", a big advantage, but in strokes 3 and 4 we had to get there from our previous stroke, and, therefore, had to be accurate

in our effort to get on the h-b line. Whenever we play to leave a h-b loser, and do not succeed in getting on the line, we have recourse to "Side" or force (i.e. a stroke made with extra power) in order to make the loser. If the angle is wider than h-b, we use "running" Side or a forcing stroke; if narrower, "check" Side or a thin stroke. "Side" will be considered later on.

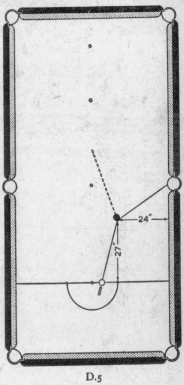

D.5

THE LONG LOSER

Stroke 1 (D.6) is the well-known "Long loser". The circle shows the area in which the o-b must lie for this stroke. The nearer it lies to the Centre Spot the better, as then both top-pkts will be available, but if it lies to one side, then, of course, the wider angle will invariably be the one to choose, unless the narrower one permits a true h-b stroke. Losers from hand with the o-b higher up the table, i.e. beyond the Pyramid Spot and well to the side of it, are also, in effect, Long losers, but the term is invariably applied to those from within the circle, and others, higher up the table, are more correctly described as "long in-offs". The ideal Long loser, of course, is from the Centre Spot. Now this stroke is, I may tell you, the

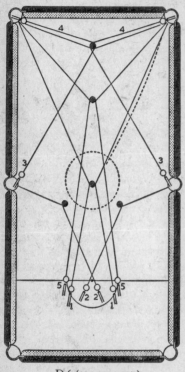

D.6 (see page 197)

most valuable practice stroke in the game; firstly, because it is the h-b stroke *at a distance* (requiring, therefore, absolute precision of aim); and, secondly, because it is an exacting test of correct cueing. Furthermore, the need for it is constant in any game. The red ball is only spotted on the Centre Spot when it has been potted twice running off its own spot and, of course, losing hazard play, as a scoring force, is always preferable with the red because it scores 3 to the white's 2. The object white is spotted on the Centre Spot when the c-b and o-b touch, and when spotting the balls after a foul. In practis-

ing the Long loser, however, we do so with the red placed on the Centre Spot, as, having mastered it from there (the ideal position), it is easy to adjust our placing of the c-b for the stroke when the o-b (red) lies off the Centre Spot, that is, in the area of the circle (D.6). In fact, so long as the position of the red allows of the h-b angle, into the top-pkt, the Long loser may be made with assurance. If it comes to rest from the previous stroke within an inch or two (on either side) of the Centre Spot, the Long loser is "on" into both top-pkts. With regard to the after-position (from the Long loser) the aim is to leave a mid-pkt loser. The broken curved line (see D.6), stroke 1, depicts the swerving course actually taken by the c-b. As I have implied, in actual play the o-b rarely stops on the Centre Spot itself, but this primary form of the Long loser is "on" from anywhere within the dotted circle, but preferably, of course, on or near it.

Cue-action for the Long loser must be free and flowing; there must be a good follow-through of the cue-wielding arm; the cue must follow a strictly horizontal line; the cue itself must be permitted to supply the force needed; cue-contact must be dead centre (though a shade of "Top", i.e. hitting one's ball above centre) may be employed—Top supplies additional momentum—and, of course, you aim through the c-b centre to the central edge of the o-b. As to spotting for the correct angle, your practice of the stroke in D.5 will have accustomed your eye to this half-angle which, in course of time, will become automatic. The ideal place for spotting the c-b in the Long loser (with o-b on Centre Spot) is on the "D" circle and about 6 in. from the Baulk-line. It is always well to take a slightly wide rather than a slightly narrow angle, and you should try to contact the o-b a trifle on the "full" side, i.e. a shade more than the exact h-b angle.

This Long loser, the one-ball exercise (plain ball, over the central spots and back, see p. 29), and the h-b loser (D.5) are all so important that proficiency at them represents a giant stride forward. Reverting to D.6, all these losers embody perfectly the h-b angle, and if the o-b is on any part of these lines, or even a trifle off them, the stroke is still a perfect h-b one.

Although in losing hazard play we enjoy a slightly greater margin of error than in winning hazard play, so far as the actual stroke is concerned, we must still aim at perfect accuracy, because breaks are not possible without accurate positioning for the next stroke. Now it so happens that the h-b loser, in most cases, destroys position instead of leaving it. Looking at D.5 you will notice that this h-b stroke sent the o-b off at a diagonal angle; in other words, towards the side of the table where it would end up outside the area of loser play. To keep within the latter, we have to keep the o-b from going to the side of the table when we make a mid-pkt loser like this one. Why then is the h-b angle so vital, you may ask?

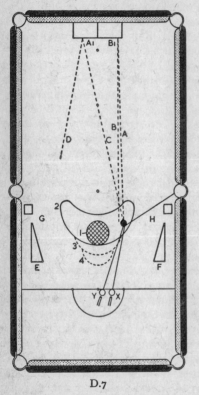

D.7

THE THICK RUN-THROUGH LOSER (D.7)

Well, it is so because, as I said previously, we are able to judge whatever contact we want by our knowledge of this angle. What we have to do, therefore, to ensure a succession of mid-pkt losers, is to make the o-b travel to the top cushion as straight as we can so that it comes back fairly *straight* and inside the upward line, *A*; if it returns nearer the "centre line" of the table, all the better, as we shall then have choice of either mid-pkt. The strength must be such as to ensure its return to area 1, or thereabouts. D.7 illustrates this. In the stroke shown, we must not send the o-b (the red) in direction

C, to rebound to D, but in direction A, to rebound along line B. If we make the stroke purely a h-b one (spotting at X), the course C—D will result. But if we spot at Y, and aim *fuller than h-b* (as you see, our knowledge of the precise h-b contact here proves its value), we contact the red fuller than h-b (almost ¾-b) and make the loser by a *run-through* stroke. This causes the red to go *straight* up the table and come back *straight*. (In both strokes, the o-b is presumed to rebound off the top cushion.) Naturally, it will not come back straight if it does not start off straight. As stated, however, a slight deviation to the left of line B will be all to the good. What we must not do is to bring the c-b back to the right of line A·

The reader then should place the red ball for a h-b losing hazard, spot the c-b to make the angle narrower than h-b, and contact the red quite thickly, i.e. practically ¾-b contact. In practising this stroke, concentrate at first on making the pocket, and then, when you have found it fairly frequently, concentrate on ensuring the straight (or almost straight) run-up of the red ball, taking the pocket for granted. Aim to contact the top cushion at the area marked $B1$; if playing on the opposite mid-pkt, the area $A1$. Follow-through with the cue, and make a free, moving stroke, without Side. You can check your spotting position by the line the red takes. Practise this thick run-through again and again, and when you have mastered it, you will have mastered one of the most valuable strokes in the game. To "run through" a ball, by the way, is to make the c-b occupy (i.e. travel over), partially or wholly, the position occupied by the o-b (D.17). This run-through loser enables us to bring the o-b ball to the mid-pkt loser area for another mid-pkt loser. Some of a series of these losing hazards may be made by an actual h-b stroke, but the majority must be run-through strokes. The indispensable thing, do not forget, is to keep the o-b *in the centre of the table*, and to play with sufficient strength to bring it back for another loser. Central position makes both mid-pkts available.

Thus losing hazard strokes may range from a pure h-b stroke to a thick ¾-b stroke, and the thick run-through, often

¾-b, is the secret of lucrative mid-pkt play. In fact, if a player mastered this stroke he would be difficult to beat, even if his other play were inferior. The requisite degree of thickness will come through experience. To keep on the mid-pkts is not easy, of course, as the required degree of strength to bring the o-b back to the mid-pkt area needs a good touch. This area is shown in D.7, section 1 (shaded) being the ideal area, section 2 the next best (it includes section 1), while sections 3 and 4 need the thickest type of run-through strokes, and these only the first-class player performs with any degree of consistency. These areas, therefore, represent the part of the table in which good mid-pkt play can be carried on. Naturally, the objective every time will be area 1 (shaded), that of the mid-pkt loser. Some players use a little check Side (l-h, in D.7 stroke) and Top for the thick run-throughs, but they *can* be, and, I advise, should be, executed without. The check Side (which I do not advise) is used because it takes the c-b well into the o-b for the thick contact. When practising these thick run-throughs, place a book on the rail opposite areas *A* and *B* (D.7) and try to make the o-b strike there. When the red ball returns on the exact centre line of the table, a loser is "on" into either pocket. If engaged in an important match, a series of losing hazards at the start will give us an idea of the pace of the table, and thus enable us to develop our strength. When we fail, through inadequate strength, to bring the o-b back for mid-pkt play, we must, of course, resort to the top-pkts, seeking by top-pkt losers to bring the o-b back for mid-pkt work, as, naturally, this is easier than using the distant pockets.

If we err and bring the o-b to the side of the bottom cushion, say, somewhere in areas *E* and *F*, we shall have to play what is called a "Short Jenny", and if in areas *G* and *H*, a "Long Jenny". These strokes will be dealt with later. If, however, we bring it to the positions shown in D.8, and others nearby, we should, with position in mind, play a different sort of loser. Thus, stroke 1: instead of a very difficult run-through, we make a very thin loser, without Side, and place the o-b for a subsequent run-through or maybe near h-b loser, as shown. In stroke 2: by a thin stroke we make the loser, and place the o-b at *B* for either a "Drop" cannon (see pp. 83–86), if white be near the Spot, or at *C*, for a top-pkt loser, the first stroke needing soft con-

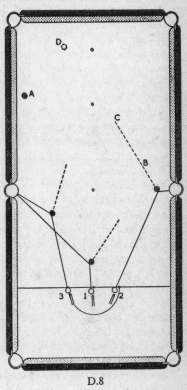

D.8

tact and slow pace, and the second, of course, a little stronger contact or pace. Stroke 3: here by a thin loser we place the o-b similarly, i.e. for a cannon or a top-pkt loser. What we must never do is to make a mid-pkt losing hazard which sends the o-b to the side of the table (except, of course, in certain cases when it is the game to do so, such as rescuing the other ball, etc.). If, for instance, the red were at *A* (D.8), we could play a h-b loser off the white into the r-h pocket to send the latter near the top cushion for a cannon, as shown by the dotted ball, thus rescuing it from a bad position.

D.9 shows: area *A*, the ideal position for mid-pkt play (plus, of course, many positions in the area no. 2 (D.7)); *B*, the area for top-pkt Long losers and long in-offs; and *C*, areas from which a long in-off, with a positional leave, is possible, should the o-b not have stopped in a better scoring area. Area *D* is that for the orthodox Long loser. As I have said, in losing hazard play (or red ball play, for that is what it amounts to, seeing that the loser off object-white counts only 2 instead of 3 for red) the primary aim is to play on the mid-pkts as long as possible, and then to use the top-pkts to

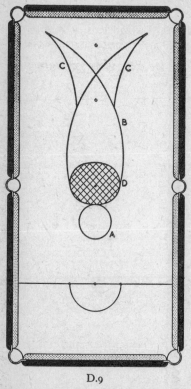

D.9

restore position on the middle, after it has been lost. That is, if we lose position in area *A* (or areas 1 and 2, D.7), we make losers into the top-pkts from area *B*, or *C* if it comes to that, to get back to area *A* (or areas 1 and 2, D.7). Area *B* includes, of course, area *D*, and the latter is the *ideal* position for the Long loser. It often happens, however, that a loser from this area does not suffice to bring the o-b back low enough for the mid-pkt losers; consequently, we must keep on with these Long losers till we do succeed in bringing the o-b (i.e. the red) low enough down the table. We should never try to

achieve such an object in one stroke, as it were, and this applies to every kind of positional objective. What two or three strokes will achieve should not be attempted in one; in other words, we need never try short-cuts in Billiards. The better our ball control and command of strength (both of which, by the way, depend wholly on that gift of true cueing I have stressed so much), the better our positional play, and the more successful our avoidance of difficulties.

MORE ABOUT THE LONG LOSER

I have said that although the h-b stroke is, so to speak, the basis of ball contacts, it is seldom employed in pure form, that is, positional considera-tions require modifica-tion of it for the majority of strokes. Although true in most respects, this is not wholly so, for, in Long loser play, provided the o-b lies within the (most desir-able) Long loser area (area D, D.9), all such strokes, except when positional considera-tions may require a different contact, are pure h-b, a fact which alone demonstrates the importance of the h-b angle. And, of course, we could not modify this angle, which we so often have to do, if we had not such an invalu-able unit to measure with.

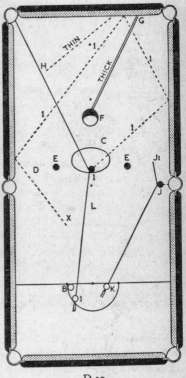

D.10 shows again this basic Long loser (1) and,

D.10

approximately, the path taken by the red ball, which may finish, say, at X for a mid-pkt loser. As there is a certain margin of error, so to speak, in the h-b contact, it is not possible to foresee the exact stopping-place of the o-b, for a thick or thin h-b contact will, of course, effect a correspondingly slight change of direction in the course of the o-b, but, generally speaking, a Long loser from this area brings the o-b to the centre of the table, and suitable for either another Long loser or, better, a mid-pkt loser. The pace of the stroke also will affect the position. Sometimes the o-b will come to rest at a spot just too far up the table for a mid-pkt loser, i.e. just below the Centre Spot, say at *L*, and the Long loser, in this case, is more difficult, needing a wider angle to effect it, so we then spot the c-b at *B*, but still make the stroke a h-b one, though slightly thicker than pure h-b, to avoid sending the o-b too near the top-pkt corner, and also to bring it well into the middle. It will, however, probably stop at *D*. If the o-b is at *E*, on either side of the Spot, or thereabouts, there is a risk of sending it into the mid-pkt; play this type of stroke, therefore, at half pace to leave the o-b near the Pyramid Spot.

By studying and carefully observing the path taken by the o-b in all types of Long loser strokes, the student will gradually learn the correct policy to pursue. Starting with the basic Long loser (from the Centre Spot), he must shift the o-b to different places, repeat each stroke a number of times and note (every student of the game should keep a note-book) the resting-place of the o-b.

In Long loser play, when the o-b lies within or round about the area *F*, particularly the black portion, the danger exists of what are called the 4-shot (white) and the 6-shot (red), that is, besides making the loser, we may pot, unintentionally, the white or red. Potting the white is, of course, disastrous, for it remains in the pocket and we have only the red left; if, however, we pot the red, the after-position, with the red placed on its Spot, may be very awkward, and we shall have lost our losing hazard position. Such strokes are called the "breeches stroke". The remedy, of course, is to contact the o-b more thickly or thinly. Thicker contact is the better way, as the o-b (in a loser from the left of the "D") will then strike the top cushion somewhere about G, as shown by the double line, whereas, if we make thin contact it will travel, off the side and top cushions, towards H, as shown, and be out of play. But if we use some check Side (r-h in this case, i.e. playing from the left of the "D"), and contacting the o-b more *thickly* than h-b, the latter will strike the cushion at G as stated, and off the side cushion come into the centre. Even good players often fall into this trap, and make the breeches stroke. It is, therefore, well worth practising avoidance of the blunder in the manner described.

If, in making the Long loser from E (either side of the Centre Spot, or indeed from some other position) we leave the red over the pocket, as at $\mathcal{J}$, we must pot it, but, instead of spotting at the opposite side of the "D", we spot at K, and then, with the red now on its Spot, we are on the h-b line, at $\mathcal{J}1$, for the subsequent loser off the spotted red. Mediocre players spot the other end of the "D", B, to get into easier position, and thus either follow-in after it or send the c-b on to the side cushion. By making this pot, an angular (though harder) one, instead of a straight one, we make the subsequent loser (from $\mathcal{J}1$) a h-b one, and thus get on the h-b line and nearer to the red into the bargain.

THE ONE-BALL PRACTICE STROKE

It is paradoxical that what at first sight would appear to be superlatively easy, that is, to send the c-b, from the middle spot of the "D", up and down the table in such a way that it travels over the Centre, Pyramid and Billiard Spots, going and returning, to end by also travelling over the centre spot of the "D", whence it started, is actually a very difficult stroke. The reason why it is very difficult is that it demands absolute central contact on the c-b (called plain-ball striking). The reward will be accurate or true cueing, the *sine qua non* of Billiards skill. The least deviation from central striking (that is, striking the c-b with the cue-tip exactly at its middle) will impart Side, and cause it to return wide of the "D" spot. All professionals and first-class amateurs practise this stroke regularly. Follow-through with the cue and make sure that your tip, at the finish of the stroke, descends slowly to the cloth and does not ascend into the air. Do the stroke with a free, flowing rhythm. This, done at various speeds, and the Long loser, with the red on the Centre Spot, are the most valuable practice strokes in Billiards. In other words, the art of plain striking (true cueing) should be mastered before Side is attempted. It is learning to walk before trying to run. I interpolate this one-ball stroke here because it is not only of immense value for achieving mastery in the game as a whole, but also because Long loser play, itself so vital, requires this art of striking the c-b without Side for its accurate execution.

THE WINNING HAZARD, OR POTTING

The statement is often made that potting is difficult because you can pot the o-b only by contacting it on one spot, namely, that dead opposite to the pocket. This is not true, because the pocket opening is, necessarily, bigger than the ball; therefore, in the pot, too, a margin of error must exist, though admittedly less than that applying to losing hazards and cannons (leaving positional requirements out of the matter). Consequently, it follows that a slight inaccuracy of contact will not cause the pot to fail. Nevertheless, the margin of error is minute, and only consistent accuracy makes the good potter. In the Top-of-the-table game and in Snooker, particularly, one cannot afford to miss more than an occasional pot against first-class players.

There are certain mental "aids" or "guides" recommended in potting, such as: (1) imagining another ball to be touching the ball to be potted and to be lying in a straight line with it and the pocket; by aiming to displace the imaginary ball with the c-b the pot can be made; (2) hitting the spot on the o-b on which you would place your cue-tip, if you were intending to send it into the pocket with your cue; (3) imagining the pocket to be 3 or 4 in. away from the o-b, that is, bringing it (with the eye, so to speak) near to the ball to be potted; (4) imagining a line drawn from the edge of the c-b to the necessary point of contact on the o-b, and making the former travel along that line to the point of contact D.11 (2) (this, of course, applies to the thin "cut" only); (5) (see D.11) imagining a line from the centre of the pocket to, and through, the o-b, so that it protrudes on the outer side of the o-b by exactly half a ball's diameter, which point B should thus be that of the c-b's centre at the moment of contact with the o-b; the aim, of course, is through the centre A of the c-b, to the end of the protruding line, B (see D.11), so that the c-b's centre,

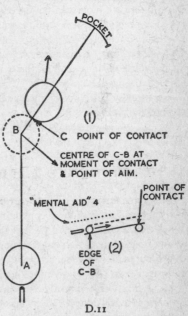

A, and its centre at the moment of contact, B, i.e. the point at which the imaginary line terminates, coincide. This expedient is perhaps the most useful, particularly as it embodies the actual theory of the pot. *The mistake many players make is to aim at* C, the point of contact, instead of at B, the c-b's centre at the moment of impact, for clearly, as the diagram shows, the points of aim and contact cannot be identical. Aiming at C would send the o-b, not to the pocket, but in the direction of the arrow. These "aids" may well prove useful to some players, and, as stated, No. 5 is in reality the actual theory of the pot, but the others are not at all a sovereign recipe for potting, and even 5, though it is indispensable in that it makes clear what we must do, does not ensure success of itself. The first-class potter has become so by long and regular practice, by cultivating true cueing and by long familiarity with angles and contacts. Nevertheless, get 5 well into your head, as every pot depends on its realization. The vast majority of first-class players pot by aiming to contact the spot on the o-b diametrically opposite to the centre of the pocket (except, of course, when the pocket is "blind" i.e. but partially accessible to the ball). In the latter case, they aim at sending the o-b towards the farther jaw.

It stands to reason that potting requires the utmost steadiness of stance and firmness of bridge. And, as in all strokes of Billiards or Snooker, it is imperative to *stay down on the stroke*, that is, not to move until it is completed. And, of course, *true cueing*, that fundamental maxim, must operate.

In full-ball pots, of course, that is when the c-b and o-b are both in a straight line with the pocket, aim is through the centres of both balls. As, however, we move away from the straight-line pot, the matter of allowing for the difference between the points of aim and contact comes into the picture, as we saw in D.11. In all such pots, and most pots are off the straight, we have to aim through the centre of the c-b at a point half a ball's diameter from the point of contact, as explained in relation to D.11.

It is a paradox that although the straight pot is theoretically the easiest of all pots, players, if some little distance is involved, often miss it. This is where true cueing comes in again, and it is well to practise straight pots with the c-b some distance from the o-b. So, put the red (or, if you are a Snooker player, the Blue) on the Centre Spot, the c-b behind it and two feet away, and practise potting the o-b into the l-h top-pkt. At first, play a plain-ball stroke, and afterwards strike the c-b low and try to stun it, so that it remains near the place of contact (see "Stun", p. 57). Strike centrally, and with some force. If you can practise with a friend, you will be spared the trouble of replacing the balls; if not, do not shirk the latter, for no progress is possible without hard work.

I now give (D.12) two valuable potting exercises, the idea of which the diagram makes quite clear. *A.* Red on Centre Spot: do the straight pot first (plain ball, i.e. without Side), then work round on each side till the "cut" pot is reached; do each pot half a dozen times. Unless practising with a friend, use the Snooker set (if available) to save labour. *B.* Red on Pyramid Spot: The same exercise as *A*, except that the top-pkt is used. Later, increase the distance between o-b and c-b.

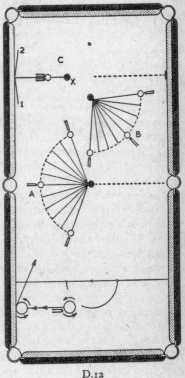

I give next a little exercise which you *must not attempt* till you become fairly efficient in "Screw"; I give it here as it comes into both potting and cannoning, and it is also a most

D.12

valuable one for both games. Place the red at X (C, D.12), and the c-b about 4 in. from it. Then put a book or some article on the cushion opposite, as shown. Apply screw-back effect, and direct the red straight to the centre of the book which represents a pocket. Next, apply r-h side, and the c-b after striking the near cushion will rebound to the *left*; then l-h side, when the rebound will be to the right. If this puzzles you, glance at the diagram ("Baulk" end), and you will see that the c-b, with r-h side, is spinning from right to left, as shown, when it reaches the cushion (and, of course, *vice versa* with

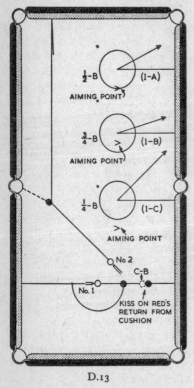

D.13

l-h side). You will realize that in each case, with the spin operating laterally, the ball *must* take the course described. This stroke will serve you well in Billiards for gathering cannons, particularly, and in Snooker for positional purposes.

D.13. No. (1) of this exercise will be found very valuable as it is a test of accurate cueing in *plain striking*, the Baulk-line providing the proof. (1) Place the red on the r-h spot of the "D", the c-b on the centre spot of the "D" or farther away if you like, now strike the red full, to make it rebound along the line from the side cushion and "kiss" the c-b full as the latter

advances, this is equivalent to a full-ball pot; (2) same position of c-b and red, i.e. the Baulk line, aim to contact the red ball at its edge, which is our old friend, the h-b stroke, note well the angle of reflection of the red, which will be that of the h-b pot; (3) same position, aim at a point on the red half-way between its centre and edge (point C in D.3), paying again special attention to the path of the red ball; a ¾-b stroke, and a ¾-b pot; (4) aim at a point the same distance *outside* the red as you did inside it in (3) (which was halfway between centre and edge—point *D* in D.3); this is a ¼-b stroke, and a ¼-b pot. When I use the word "pot" in these instances, I do not mean an actual pot, as you are not playing at a pocket, but the course given the red ball corresponds to that taken by it in such pots. By noting the direction of the red in each of these strokes, i.e. (2), (3) and (4), you will be enabled to memorize them, which will serve you extremely well in positional play, and in potting at both games, Billiards and Snooker. Now turn to 1*A*, 1*B* and 1*C*.

The arrow and line (centre of ball to cushion) in each case form an angle which shows the course, approximately, taken by the o-b in: (1*A*) the h-b pot; (1*B*) the ¾-b pot, and (1*C*)the ¼-b pot, angles which, as I have said, *you should memorize*. The inverted arrows indicate the points of aim for these contacts, but these you will have already learned. It goes without saying that you should do each stroke a number of times before going on to the next one. One more valuable potting exercise is the other stroke on D. 13, No. 2. Place the red as shown, pot it from a similar angle from the "D"— the red ball prevents its being placed there in the diagram— and send the c-b up the table to rebound from the cushion, in position for potting the red off the Billiard Spot.

D.14 shows a few pots of special significance. Nos. 1 and 1ᴬ illustrate the need for adjustment of aim in very *slow* pots into a mid-pkt, with (1) and against the nap (1ᴬ). These pots are often missed (particularly in Snooker) owing to the player's disregard of nap effect (see pp. 45–51). In each case *A* represents what should be the line of aim, and *B* the path of the o-b. As shown, with the nap, the o-b drifts towards the top end of the table; against the nap, the drift is to the Baulk end. It is with slow strokes that this must be specially taken into account. Stroke 2 is a kiss-pot: contacting the red ball fully, the latter kisses the c-b directly after contact, and is diverted into the pocket, thereby enabling the c-b to remain on the h-b line for the cross loser into the opposite pocket; if the red is cut in, the c-b, naturally, must come away to the right. Many players either do not know this pot or fear to make it; it is easy and cannot be missed. In stroke 3 we pot the red, and,

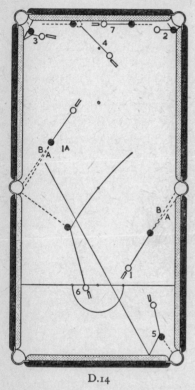

D.14

with strong r-h (running) Side, run-through on to the cushion on to the h-b line for the cross loser. Stroke 4 is a cushion pot, and one very important in both games (again, particularly in Snooker). To effect this pot the c-b must strike the cushion and the red almost simultaneously; I say almost, as the aim should be to contact the cushion a fraction before the o-b, the latter being potted off the far shoulder; running (l-h here) Side should be used, although the pot can be made without it, but it is always used, and it probably imparts speed to the o-b when the cushion *is* struck a second, so to speak, before the o-b, and promotes a squarish contact: the stroke can be made at other angles approximating to the one shown. Stroke 5 is a simple pot with a little running (r-h) Side to send the c-b to the mid-pkt area for the cross loser (i.e. h-b) off the red (on its spot). Stroke 6 is a slow angular pot into the left mid-pkt, with some running (r-h) Side to direct the c-b to a position to make the h-b loser off the red. Stroke 7: here the two balls, c-b and o-b, are both touching the cushion; gentle-paced stroke, without Side, aim being through the centres of both balls. It is difficult to make the c-b follow-on into the pocket (if needed) with this pot, as the pace necessary may spoil the pot.

D.15 depicts a few positional pots. (1) This pot is very important (I gave a form of it before, D.10 (*J*)). Instead of potting the red by a straight pot (that is, by spotting at the r-h end of the "D", in order to "make it easy"), we spot to make it an angle pot, and aim to make the c-b rest on the h-b line (see arrow), for the cross loser off the red (on its spot); if we make the pot straight (easy), we run the risk of running into the pocket, or causing the c-b to come to rest against the pocket jaw(s); this is a most important stroke.

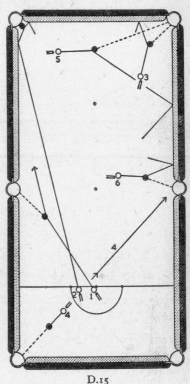

D.15

(2) By a cushion-first slow stroke we cut the red in and, using Bottom, remain on the cross loser (h-b) line or, at worst, get behind the red (on its spot) for a pot; Bottom is always needed when we are seeking to reduce the pace of the c-b. (3) Again we pot the red, with check (r-h) Side, and, using Bottom, come to rest on the h-b angle. (4) A screw-back pot to get to the

mid-pkt area for the cross loser (line 4 shows the ball's path); we may send the c-b into the pocket but that cannot be helped; to pot the red, and follow-on, would bring the same result as if the c-b went into the mid-pkt by the screw-back, but by making the latter stroke we have a good chance of leaving the c-b in break position, and either by the h-b cross loser or a forcing stroke, getting in off the red (on its spot). (5) When potting the red here, we send the c-b off the side cushion on to the h-b loser line. (6) Again the same object; here, however, we must use strong check (r-h) Side, to bring the c-b as *straight* as possible back off the cushion for the h-b loser. These strokes emphasize the need always to place the c-b in loser position after potting the red.

CANNONS

We can make a cannon by a ball-to-ball stroke, which is a direct cannon; by a ball-cushion-ball stroke (indirect) and by a cushion-first (i.e. cushion-ball-ball) stroke. The h-b stroke enters into cannon play, as it does into losing hazards. A great number of cannons are made by h-b contact, but, of course, there are countless positions in which this contact must be modified (as with loser play), and countless others in which the cannon is not possible by h-b contact.

To make a cannon with the balls in cannon position is, of course, simple; to make it, to satisfy positional needs, not at all simple. The majority of amateurs treat the cannon merely as a means of obtaining loser position, and ignore the intrinsic possibilities of cannon play, by which I mean that (1) it is often possible to make more than one cannon, with the balls close (I am not referring to "Nurseries", see p. 128) and thus score additional points; (2) by care in contact on both the object balls, instead of merely placing one for the losing hazard or pot, and ignoring the other, both balls can be kept under control. It is, of course, not easy to contact both the o-b's as desired, but by constant regard to positional play in general, and by practising accuracy of contact in cannon play, it becomes easier.

In Continental Billiards, the type without pockets, scoring is by cannon play alone and, of course, the players develop remarkable skill in cannon play. Naturally, there being no pockets on the Continental table, cannon play is facilitated; nevertheless, I do think that cannon play might be exploited in English Billiards to a far greater extent than it is. In any case, amateurs, in general, would without doubt improve their game considerably, and make bigger breaks, by concentrating far more than they do (if, in the generality of cases they do so at all) on the positional aspects of cannon play. In other words, they would do well to bring into the matter of ball contacts in cannon play something of the precision they are compelled to exercise in winning and losing hazards.

Another way in which the amateur might exploit further cannon play is by using the cushions far more than he does. Most players ignore the cushion and its incalculable value for cannon play and, as it were, treat the cushions as merely objects to keep the balls on the table. A great cannon player like Clark McConachy, of New Zealand, on the contrary, enlists the aid of the cushions in his cannon play to a remarkable extent.

Many cannons are traps for the unwary, and, in fact, indifferent or inaccurate cannon play is often the cause of breaks coming to a premature end. I do not suggest that being careful about the after-position of one of the two o-b's only, in a cannon, is bad Billiards. Far from it, but it is not the best Billiards, and early cultivation of the practice of looking after the second object ball (when, say, the first has been placed for a losing hazard, or *vice versa*) and of trying to make purposeful contact on both o-b's will help towards attaining a high standard.

D.16 shows four cannons in which both object balls are taken into account. No. 1 is a h-b stroke; by using the cushion we place red over the centre-pkt, and send white gently in position for a mid-pkt loser. No. 2 looks simple but it is not.

The h-b stroke would make the c-b contact red on the farther (i.e. wrong) side, as the broken line shows, and send the object white "safe" (dash-dot line); we should contact the white very full, to send it near the Spot, and use all possible r-h (running) Side to allow for this full contact and to get a little to the right of red, so that, in potting it into the mid-pkt, we can go up the table with the c-b for Top-of-the-table play. The Side will prevent the c-b striking red on the left, its wrong side for our going up the table after the pot. This stroke illustrates the subtle side of Billiards and the need for discrimination in cannon play. By the h-b stroke we *might* succeed in leaving a top-pkt loser off white, but it would be doubtful: good Billiards does not consist of "mights". Stroke 3: Here we have a soft screw cannon: we contact white fully, and send it to the Spot off the cushions, use a little check (r-h) Side to drop on red centrally (and *not* to the left, which might happen with running (l-h) or no Side at all), and thus direct the red pocketwards. Stroke 4: A run-through cannon, sending red, off two cushions, towards the top-pkt area, and pushing white a little forward for a loser either next stroke, or, after potting

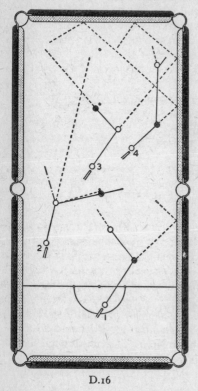

D.16

red, by leaving the c-b on the top cushion (for the white loser). These cannons will serve to illustrate the art of making purposeful contact on both balls (whenever possible) in cannon play. Although you may be unable to place both balls advantageously in a cannon, and may have to concentrate on one only, you should take the position of the other into your stroke and plan, and not leave it out of account. D.17 shows how a run-through stroke, causing the c-b to follow in the path, more or less, of the o-b, permits the cannon when the h-b

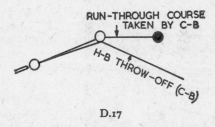

RUN-THROUGH COURSE
TAKEN BY C-B

H-B THROW-OFF (C-B)

D.17

stroke would carry the c-b wide of the o-b. The way to gauge the contact for a plain-ball run-through cannon is to visualize the line the c-b would take if it followed straight in the track of the first o-b, and then to alter the contact from full ball according to the position of the second o-b. In the stroke shown, the contact on the first o-b would be a trifle to the right of full, as the second o-b lies to the right. Some "Top" (see p. 42) is useful for carrying the c-b forward after the "shock" of collision with o-b No. 1. The run-through should always err on the side of fullness than the reverse.

SIDE

I am not exaggerating at all when I say that the excessive use, or rather, the abuse, of Side is an important reason why thousands of amateurs remain mediocre players. In other words, all these players are not striking the c-b where they

think they are. I have stressed the enormous importance of
plain striking, or striking without Side, and of the importance
of being able to hit a ball *straight* up and down the table,
making it come back to the spot whence it started. When you
can do this with a marked degree of success, you are fitted to
study and use Side, but not before!

Side is a most valuable servant, but the worst of masters,
in Billiards; it is also a complex matter, and, therefore, well
worth serious study. What is Side? Simply spin, and it is
imparted, administered, employed, applied, put on (to enumer-
ate the various terms used), by a crisp, deft and decisive blow
of the cue on one side or the
other of the c-b. D.18 (1)
illustrates the points of contact for imparting the various
types of spin or lateral rotation.

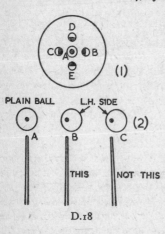

D.18 (1): The circle *A*
shows our point of contact
for plain-ball striking, i.e.
no Side; circle *B*, that for
imparting r-h side; circle
C, that for l-h side; circle
D, that for applying Top
(extra forward rotation or
spin); and *E*, the contact
point for Bottom (checking
forward rotation), Drag (a slither of the c-b, delaying forward rotation and functioning of Side), and the Screw and
Screw-back strokes (the latter resulting in backward recoil).
The dark part of each circle is that actually contacted by
the tip, for, the ball being round, the tip gets near to full
contact in plain-ball striking only, and then even as the tip
itself is round, there is nothing like full contact. A player
skilled in using Side can venture nearer the Side edge of the
c-b for applying right and left Side, but enough Side for most
purposes may be applied by contacting the small circular spots

shown, the shaded portions representing the actual tip contacts, as stated.

In applying Side, it is all-important that the axis of the cue (i.e. the line from tip to butt) be exactly parallel, at the moment of striking, to its position when the stroke is a plain one (i.e. struck at its centre), as the cue *B* is parallel to cue *A*, D.18 (2). It is also essential that the cue be kept horizontal. If these two requisites are not kept in mind, the line of aim will be wrong. In a word, the cue must be kept straight which means that if you strike the c-b a little to the right of its centre, then you must move your bridge the same distance to the right from its position for central aim. Also you must not tilt it. Why is Side necessary? The answer is: to enlarge (by running Side) or diminish (by check Side) the angle of the c-b's divergence from a plain-ball stroke. There are two other ways of doing this: by Screw, and the "forcing" stroke, but Screw cannot be controlled in pace and direction so accurately as Side, and forcing shots, of course, serve only for a limited number of strokes. Side then is the means whereby the angles resulting from plain-ball strokes, and $\frac{1}{4}$-b, h-b and $\frac{3}{4}$-b contacts, can be modified.

D.19 (1) shows the effect of Side, compared with plain-ball striking. The stroke shown is a cushion cannon. The plain (h-b) stroke leaves the cushion after contact with the first o-b in direction *A*; applying running Side, it leaves the cushion in direction *B*, applying check (r-h) Side, direction is as shown, *C*. Now, if we are faced with this cannon, by experience we shall know that the plain-ball stroke will miss the second o-b, coming off the cushion, as we see, at too narrow an angle; check Side will narrow the angle of reflection still more, and, of course, we should never think of using it, unless the o-b were at *Z*. Knowing the h-b angle of reflection, we see that, to effect the cannon, we must widen the angle quite a lot, so we apply plenty of running (l-h here) Side and make the cannon, as shown at *B*. The amount of Side to be used becomes known to us through experience and practice.

You will have noticed I have employed two new terms,

running and check Side. These correspond to "angle-widening" and "angle-narrowing" Side, and may be either r-h or l-h, according to the position. "Running" probably derives from the lively speed at which a ball, laden with running Side,

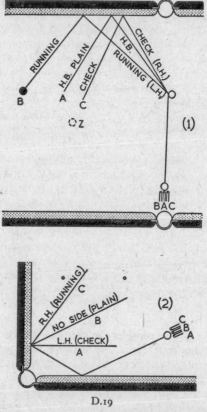

D.19

darts off a cushion, and "check" from the way in which the c-b is retarded or "checked" in cushion contact when such Side is used. D.19 (2) also shows the properties of Side, as compared with plain-ball striking.

A good practice stroke for the application of Side is the following: Place the c-b on the l-h spot of the "D", and aim, by a plain-ball stroke to send it along the Baulk-line, towards the r-h cushion so that it returns on the line (if it does, your cueing will be admirable!). Now strike it to the right, applying r-h side (see D.18 (1)); afterwards, from the other side of the "D", to the left, applying l-h side. The test of whether you can apply Side well will be (taking the r-h side stroke) your ability to make the c-b contact the bottom cushion. If you do this stroke from the other side of the table, you should also aim at making the c-b contact the bottom cushion (with, this time, l-h side). If you can get near the bottom cushion with these Side strokes you will be doing very well indeed.

Side should be imparted by a *deftly* executed blow of the tip at the points, C and B, indicated in D.18 (1), i.e. about half-way between the ball's middle and edge, and at half the ball's height. As you strike, bear in mind that you are wanting to make the ball spin well from right to left, or left to right, as required. Concentrate on your tip's function, ensuring that it grips the ball's surface well and imparts the spin. Keep your cue level! Chalk your cue always before putting on Side! Do not try to strike the "outside edge"; you will only miscue. And remember, a "deft" blow does not mean a purely forceful one. The stroke is just a lively tap, in which the cue is quickly withdrawn.

The Nap

We have now to consider the effects of the nap of the cloth in conjunction with Side. The nap runs from the Baulk area to the other end (the "Spot" or top end) of the table. There are 15,000 threads from the Baulk end to the top, and each is made up of a mass of tiny fibres, every one of which, in its turn, is built up of delicate microscopic cells, each fitting into and overlapping, the other, and very much resembling the scales of fish. This nap, therefore, exercises in all medium- and slow-paced strokes a decided effect on the running of the c-b. In D.19, the strokes were, more or less, across the table, and straight across the table the nap's influence is negligible. In fast strokes, the pace discounts nap effects. In slow and medium strokes, the nap in conjunction with Side, exercises strong influence. If, with your hand, you stroke the cloth, first towards the top, then towards the bottom end, you will realize, from the smoothness in the first instance, and the rough, resistant touch in the second, why nap affects the run of a ball, to which Side has been applied. Without Side, the nap effect is negligible. D.20 shows the effects, in a slow or medium stroke, of running and check Side, and plain (h-b) ball after contact with another ball. In stroke B, the running Side effect is stimulated by the nap; in stroke D, the check Side is slightly countered by the nap.

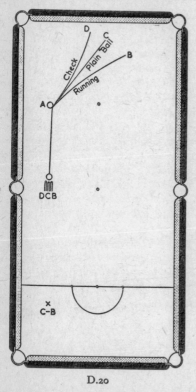

D.20

It is in running Side effects that the nap acts most. The Side administered begins to act, of course, before contact, as we shall see; this is in slow and medium strokes in which the c-b travels a fair distance. If, in D.20, the c-b started its course at X, and with running (r-h) Side, and the aim were h-b, the pre-contact pull of the Side would, assisted by the nap, result in an almost $\frac{1}{4}$-b contact. Consequently, we must allow for this, so that, if we desire a h-b contact, as here, we must, in slow and medium strokes, with running Side, aim for a fuller than h-b contact, let us say, a $\frac{3}{4}$-b one. If the desired contact were $\frac{1}{4}$-b, then we must, with running Side, aim for h-b. Conversely, if using check Side, we must, if intending h-b contact, aim for $\frac{1}{4}$-b, and so on. The effect of Side up the table (i.e. with the nap) increases in proportion as the pace used is lessened.

Let us now see what happens when we play against the nap. In a fast stroke again, the nap will not exercise any appreciable difference of direction in the c-b, the pace killing the nap effect, but with medium and slow strokes again, the nap takes effect, but, curiously, acts in a contrary way, compared with playing with the nap, that is, instead of right side causing the c-b, after contact, to veer to the right, it makes it veer to the left, and *vice versa*.

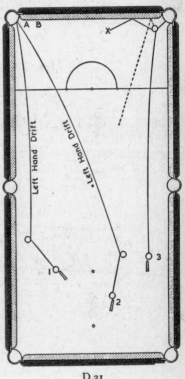

D.21

D.21 exhibits this "against-the-nap" effect. Stroke 1: Contrary to when we play this slow long in-off with the nap, we use r-h side, contact the white h-b, and the c-b, instead of turning to the right, as with the nap, drifts to the left; our aim should, therefore, be at *A* (pocket-shoulder); contact should be h-b or thinner, according to the position. Stroke 2: A similar sort of stroke, with h-b contact, and again we use r-h side, and aim at *B*, and the Side will cause the c-b to veer towards and enter the pocket. Stroke 3: Here the loser-angle off the o-b (white) is narrow so that, unless we make a very thin stroke (which, however, we should not do, as the white will then probably remain in baulk in *X* direction), we must effect a run-through, and this we do by aiming almost *full* ball, with plenty of l-h side which will cause the c-b to veer to the right and make a thick h-b contact, ensuring the run-through loser. If we played a fast stroke accurate contact would be difficult and we could not control the white ball, which we seek to position for a mid-pkt loser, and if we played a very fast skimming stroke we should probably send the white to the left, for it to remain in Baulk. So we play a nice slow-paced stroke on the lines stated.

As we saw in stroke 3, D.21, we have to make the same allowance in aiming, for slow strokes, and slow-medium, for the pull of the Side in against-the-nap positions, when the c-b has some distance to run, as in with-the-nap strokes. Drag (see p. 58) is useful in these slow strokes, with and against the nap, and it, to a great extent, obviates having to counter the (pre-contact) pull away effect of the Side (in conjunction with the nap) by modification of aim. As the reader will see later, Drag preserves the effect of Side for a considerable distance, the latter starting to operate when the drag effect ceases; consequently, as the c-b will then be fairly near the o-b, there will not be so much, if indeed any scope, for it to run-off or deviate from the intended line of aim.

D.22: To illustrate further the nap effects, here is the same cannon played (stroke 1) with the nap; (stroke 2) against the nap. In each case the angle is *less than* h-b, the letter *A* (stroke 1) and *D* (stroke 2) representing the c-b position, *if* the angle were a true h-b. In stroke 1, we use check (l-h) Side, and $\frac{1}{4}$-b contact (i.e. check, to counter the narrower than h-b angle) and, as shown by the curved line, the Side pulls the c-b towards the o-b after contact, acting in conjunction with the

nap. Without the Side, the c-b would have run past red on
the r-h side. In stroke 2, knowing now that r-h side, against
the nap, will cause the c-b to veer to the left, we use it instead
of l-h, as in stroke 1, and, as shown, the c-b, after contact
veers to the left; with-
out Side, it would have
passed red on its r-h
side. I may add that
these two cannons could
be made also by a thin
or fine stroke or by a
thick run-through, but
I show them made, as
in the diagram, because
I am illustrating nap
and Side effects.

To sum up: With the
nap in slow and medium
strokes: r-h side pulls
the c-b to the right, be-
fore and after contact;
l-h to the left. Against
the nap: r-h side pulls
the c-b to the left, be-
fore and after contact;
l-h side, to the right.

Owing to the pre-
contact pulling effect of
Side, that is, in slowish
strokes, *with* the nap, we
must, when using run-

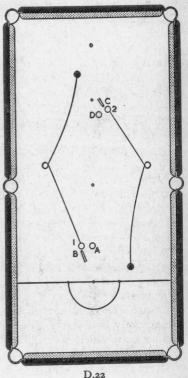

D.22

ning Side, aim more fully than for our intended contact; when
using check Side, aim finer than for our intended contact.

Owing to the pre-contact pulling effect, *against* the nap, we
must, with running Side, aim finer than for our intended contact; with check Side, aim thicker.

With fast strokes the nap effect is negligible and, in most

cases, non-existent; in slow strokes it is most pronounced; in medium strokes, less pronounced, but allowance has to be made.

Across the table the Side and nap effect is, in straight strokes, practically non-existent; in diagonal and slow strokes it operates to a limited extent.

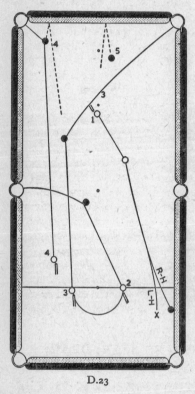

D.23

With and against the nap, it is the pulling-away tendency of the c-b before contact that has chiefly to be taken into account with Side, and, as we know, this pull is in the opposite direction to what it is, with the nap.

In strokes, against the nap, in which the c-b has but a very short distance to run before contacting the o-b, and the same distance after, either to contact the second o-b or enter a pocket, the same Side serves as with the nap. If the c-b has only a short distance to travel to contact the first o-b, but a long distance, after contact, to reach the second o-b or enter a pocket, we must employ the opposite Side to that we would use *with* the nap. D.23, 1, shows a long run-through cannon which illustrates this point. Contacting the white fully ($\frac{3}{4}$-b) with strong running (r-h) Side, Top and some pace, the c-b veers gradually to the left to effect the cannon; with l-h (check) Side, it would veer to the right (X), as shown. Strokes 2 and 3 show the strong pull of the Side (plus nap effect) in two losing hazard strokes. In stroke 2, the red is too far up the table for a plain-ball stroke; so with the utmost running Side possible, the c-b, contacting the red thickly (we aim, in accordance with what has been said, more thickly than $\frac{3}{4}$-b, i.e. almost full), curves beautifully round to enter the pocket; stroke 3 is similar; aiming thickly (almost full) we make a thick h-b contact, and the c-b drifts gradually into the r-h top-pkt, a spectacular stroke. Both strokes are medium paced. Stroke 4 is a loser, with check (r-h) Side, with the nap. Red is too close to the pocket for a plain h-b stroke (a thin stroke would send red to the side). So, aiming h-b, we achieve, by aid of the drift to the right, a $\frac{3}{4}$-b contact and thus a run-through loser. This stroke is the same as No. 3 (D.21) made against the nap, and should be compared. Strokes 2 and 3 represent the widest angles that Side (plus nap) can achieve, and they must be made at quite slow pace, as it is, as stated, at such pace that Side acts most powerfully with the nap. With the o-b at 5 (see D.23), by spotting at the l-h spot of the "D", and using all the Side we can (r-h, running), we can, by a slow stroke, aiming full (and thus making $\frac{3}{4}$-b contact), make the loser into the r-h top-pkt, a very wide angle which the Side and nap pull make practicable. The thick contact will ensure a fairly straight rebound of red from the top cushion, thus leaving another loser into the top l-h pocket.

SCREW; STUN AND STAB; DRAG; FORCING STROKES; TOP AND BOTTOM; FINE STROKES; THE PIQUÉ STROKE; THE SWERVE

Screw

We now come to an element of the game which is of supreme value—Screw. Screw imparts backward rotation or recoil to the c-b, that is, we are able, by it, to make the latter rebound from the o-b to any point in an arc ranging from a straight-back direction to a lateral (i.e. sideways) angle which exceeds a right angle by a few degrees. D.24 will make this clear. All the "throw-offs" shown can be obtained by the Screw Stroke.

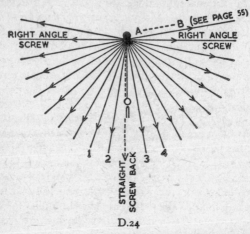

D.24

The direct rebound and angles 1, 2, 3 and 4 are called screw-back effects. Screwing back always presents difficulties to the learner, and even to quite good players. Screw is obtained by striking the c-b below its centre half-way between its centre and bottom. The reason why so many players are poor at the stroke is that, instead of following-through with the cue,

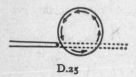

D.25

fearing they may not have time to withdraw it out of the way of the returning c-b, they snatch the cue away at the moment of impact. They also do the stroke too stiffly and clumsily. The stroke must be made with a flexible wrist action. A downward dig is fatal; and do not make any hasty movement to draw the cue back, i.e. pull it out of the way, and don't forget to keep the butt end low. The cue must, as it were, "go right through" the c-b. D.25 shows how the cue should follow-through, yet leave ample time to withdraw it out of the way of the returning c-b. As will be seen, the ball is undergoing backward spin and this operates directly the o-b is struck by it. Take care to keep the whole cue absolutely *horizontal*, and make the stroke a firm one. The bridge must, of course, be lowered. Many teachers maintain that, at the moment of impact of cue and c-b, the cue should be suddenly gripped tight, but this is not necessary, if the cue-hold is firm at the start of the stroke. Walter Lindrum, the greatest player of all time, always advocated holding the cue firmly at the *start* of the stroke, and what he says is indeed authoritative.

Remember then the most important thing in screwing is: do not check the forward action of the cue, and drive it through the c-b unhesitatingly. What you have to do is to impart the backward spin the diagram illustrates, and with this idea well in mind, the purpose of the stroke should be quite clear and practicable. Do not strike lower than the point suggested above, or you will get under the ball and simply jostle it into the air. The weight of the cue supplies the retrograde motion, and also the making of the stroke in a purposeful, clean and incisive manner.

Many players use a special (and lower) bridge for screwing purposes, the *bouclée* (see D.26A), as this method facilitates screw action, but the stroke can be made quite satisfactorily with the orthodox bridge. The *bouclée* is formed by doubling the first finger so that its tip contacts the thumb opposite its second joint, thus forming a loop through which the cue can be passed and slid to and fro. D.26B shows another low bridge which may be used for screwing.

Another fault in screwing is indecision when to strike, the player making too many motions, through not having decided how many he will make before striking. He should decide upon the number and stick to it. To move one's cue a different number of times when making this or that stroke is to court failure. So decide the matter once for all! If you decide, after experiment, that the grip on the cue should come only at the moment of impact of cue and c-b, well and good—it is,

as I said, often recommended—but I remain unconvinced of
its necessity, and prefer to grip it (not too rigidly, of course)
throughout the entire stroke. The same with wrist action; I
believe it helps considerably; some hold with it, others do
not. To sum up, with regard to this all-important stroke, the
screw-back: (1) Keep the cue horizontal; (2) follow-through

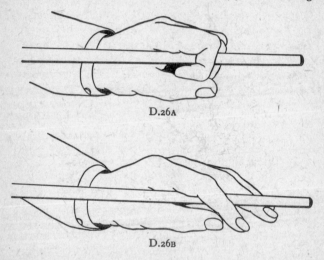

D.26A

D.26B

with the cue, say, 3 in. beyond the c-b; (3) do not snatch the
cue away: give it time to do its work, i.e. to impart backward
motion; (4) concentrate on the point of impact, and upon the
fact that you are going to make the ball revolve, as the arrows
(D.25) indicate; (5) make your stroke incisive, resolute, but
not one of brute force, as it were; the stroke should be delicate and deft; (6) follow-through with the wrist; (7) remember,
a hard stroke is not needed, except when the o-b is distant,
of course.

Screw-back strokes, of course, are only a part of the full
range of Screw shots. D.24 illustrates the various backward and lateral angles of reflection from the o-b. Any
screwing angle is executed by the same means as the direct

screw-back. Do not fall into the error of using Side to effect the countless throw-offs between the full contact on the o-b and the limit, i.e. that just beyond the right-angle throw-off. To alter the direction of the c-b's throw-off *alter your point of contact on the object ball*, hitting the c-b *centrally* every time. Side *is* used with Screw, but only for special strokes, as we shall see.

For a right-angle Screw we contact the o-b h-b, aiming, of course, at the outer edge of the o-b through the c-b's centre. Therefore, all the Screw Stroke angles in between this h-b contact on the edge of the o-b and its centre (as in the direct screw-back) can be made by points of contact lying between

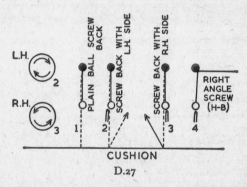

D.27

the o-b's edge and its centre. For a Screw Stroke at an angle a little greater than a right-angle (*A—B*, see D.24) we contact the o-b more thinly than h-b, but the right-angle Screw really represents more or less the limit of controlled Screw for the generality of strokes.

D.27 gives some Screw exercises. (1) A straight screw-back (put the balls far enough out from the cushion to be able to make your bridge comfortably, and practise this stroke with the orthodox and the *bouclée* bridges); (2) screw-back (straight) with l-h side; c-b will rebound off the cushion to the *right*; (3) screw-back (straight) with r-h side; c-b will rebound off cushion to the *left* (the two balls on the left show how the

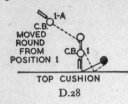

D.28

side acts against the cushion), D.28, a cannon stroke, will make the matter clear; moving the c-b round gradually from position 1 till the position 1A is reached we see that, to make the c-b travel to the right, to effect the cannon, we still employ l-h side as in the screw-back stroke; (4) a right angle, i.e. h-b screw cannon, the aim being at the o-b's edge (as by this time you know!). No Side.

Screw has often to be combined with Side but Screw by itself does not need Side for its maximum expression or range. You can get all the Screw capacity you require by central striking, and, in fact, more than you can by Screw plus Side. Side is essential, however, in a Screw Stroke when the pocket is "blind" (not open). D.29, stroke 1, shows a screw loser ($\frac{3}{4}$-b contact on its l-h side) into a blind pocket. In such strokes the c-b may easily, and, in fact, often does, strike the farther jaw, so here we apply r-h (check, or in such cases, "pocket") Side to provide for collision with the farther shoulder or jaw. Ball *A* shows how the c-b is spinning, and

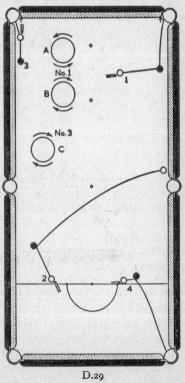

D.29

it is obvious that if we had used running (l-h) Side (*B*), or no Side at all, the o-b would have met with resistance from the pocket jaw, instead of assistance, as with pocket Side. No. 2 stroke is a curvilineal screw shot, with running (r-h) Side. To secure a curved run of the c-b, running Side plus Screw is the means. No. 3, a screw-back loser, with pocket Side. As the c-b recoils, it might contact the pocket jaw, and as l-h side (i.e. pocket Side) causes it to spin from left to right (ball *C*) it must enter the pocket from the jaw. It may do so without touching the jaw, of course, but we have to provide for the contingency, and this the pocket Side achieves. No. 4 is a screw loser, with thin contact, so as not to send the red out of range; running (r-h) Side is used, as, by its use, we mitigate the pace, and may achieve thinner contact than with Screw alone. It is a right-angle stroke, and to make it by Screw alone would need h-b contact; with Side we may hit it more thinly and thus not send the red out of control. It will be obvious that the cue cannot be kept horizontal for screwing purposes in which the c-b is near a cushion. In this case, it must, of course, be tilted, but if it is very near, then Screw is not possible.

Stun and Stab

There is not much difference between these two strokes. To Stun the c-b we hold the cue firmly, and the actual motion consists of a heavy sort of jab at the c-b, with Bottom on the latter (i.e. it is struck low down as in Screw, but with no follow-through). The o-b is given a weighty "stunning" stroke. The object of Stun and Stab is to drive the o-b a distance, whether to pot it or to drive it round the table, as in a gathering cannon, and, at the same time, to leave the c-b actually on (Stab), or near (Stun), the actual spot the o-b occupied prior to the stroke.

The stroke, in effect, "kills" pace in the c-b. The latter should be struck low, though not so low as in Screw Strokes, but there should be no Screw effect (unless to do so partially is so desired), and the cue should *not* follow-through at all.

The stroke resembles somewhat an indifferent player's attempt to screw back in that, not following through with his cue, he imparts no screw (-back) effect and so leaves the c-b stationary. An important point is that the o-b be struck full and weightily. The stroke is the one shot in Billiards (or Snooker) which should be done in a heavy-handed way, and, of course, the player must grip his cue firmly. When you wish to pot a ball lying near the pocket edge, and cause the c-b to occupy its place, you use the Stab Stroke. Also, in a gathering cannon (i.e. one which brings the three balls together), you send one ball up and down, or round, the table by stunning the c-b, so that it stays nearby, to cannon on to the other (adjacent) o-b, while the first o-b, driven by the c-b a distance (i.e. round the table), returns to the place whence it departed. The more fully the o-b is struck, the less the c-b will be moved in Stun and Stab Strokes. (See p. 164, D.10.)

Drag

This is a most valuable element in Billiards but one which only the top players are masters of. Its purpose is to slow up the pace of a stroke, and also to avoid the deviation of the c-b in a long-distance stroke which may be caused by particles of dirt, chalk, etc., which sometimes produce such deviation. Yet another advantage of Drag is that it retains the Side imparted in a long-distance stroke, *delaying its action* until it nears the o-b. It also kills the pull of the Side away from the o-b which occurs in a stroke without Drag.

What is Drag exactly? If you see anyone using it you will know at once he is a first-rate exponent of Billiards, but as few are, it follows you will not find it easy to come across one who skilfully uses Drag. Drag is achieved by striking the c-b low down, though not so low as for Screw, and instead of a follow-through with the cue, the latter is arrested or checked at the moment of contact, a rather crisp, snappy thrust being need-ful. The object is to make the c-b slide or "slither" over the cloth during the initial stage of its run. The friction of the cloth gradually slows up the c-b, helped by the suspended rotation or Drag imparted by the low-striking delivery. If Side also has been applied, it does not begin to operate, nor does forward rotation, until the Drag effect is exhausted, and during the "sliding" stage, the ball cannot deviate from its course, for it is travel-ling too fast. When the Drag effect is exhausted, the pace of the ball slows up considerably, and thus the o-b is not struck by the c-b so forcibly as it must necessarily be in a similar stroke played without Drag, a great advantage, positionally. Drag can be used with short strokes, such as a mid-pkt loser, but it is generally limited to long-distance strokes. Willie Smith, however, a very great player and a master of Drag, uses it magically in even short-distance strokes.

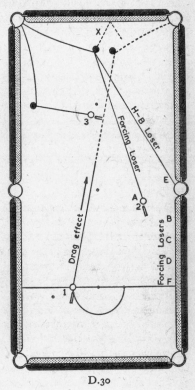

D.30

D.30, stroke 1, is a losing hazard, with Drag, the effect of which lasts, more or less, till the straight line ends, after which the strong running Side we apply (because the angle of the loser is considerably wider than the h-b angle) and the thick contact-aim (¾-b), to bring the o-b back off the cushion as straight as possible, resulting in a thick h-b contact, cause the c-b to curl round into the pocket, a very pretty stroke. We use slow to medium pace because Side operates strongly at such pace, and, because a fast stroke (forcing, with r-h side) would send the red goodness knows where! As we must always aim at ball control, it is easy to see that Drag, with its power to ensure true running in slow and medium strokes, its retention of the *full* Side influence (in a stroke without Drag, the Side operates at the outset and is, therefore, partially used up on contact), and, as the pace slows up, at the cessation of Drag influence, its power also to slow up the pace with which the o-b rebounds off the top cushion, to the benefit of positional control, it is easy to see that Drag, I repeat, is an invaluable element in refined Billiards. As you see, it eliminates the need for pace in both c-b and o-b. The effect of Drag as played by an expert is fascinating, the ball, after the Drag is exhausted, spinning away in a fascinating manner.

Forcing Strokes

When we have a loser or a cannon, the angle of which is greater than h-b, we can make the stroke by using force, and we may also add Top and Side. E (D.30) shows the basic h-b loser off the red on its spot. If, however, the c-b is at $A2$, it is clear the h-b contact will not serve, so we must make up for the difference, and this we do, by a forcing stroke, using Top and strong l-h side, but if we can do without the Side, so much the better, as, firstly, it may result in a thinner contact than required, and, secondly, because of that, it may cause the red to contact the top cushion diagonally, as shown (X), and so it will not rebound *straight* up and down the table, to the advantage of position, as we naturally wish (it may stay in Baulk, but this we seek to prevent by gauging the strength or force). In a forcing stroke, we must go right through with our cue, and, so to speak, throw the cue at the ball (do not interpret this *literally*, as our control of it must never be relinquished!). When you have executed this forcing loser a few times, try to do it, with the c-b, successively, at B, C, D and F (about the limit for the stroke). Top consists in striking the c-b at half-way between its top and centre. Stroke 3 is another forcing stroke, made with check (l-h) Side (Side is not really necessary in a forcing stroke except into a blind pocket) because it may spoil our intended contact and because the force itself, in a h-b forcer, is capable of achieving the wide angle required. Here we have a blind pocket, and, therefore,

must use some pocket Side in case the c-b strikes the far shoulder. Moreover, we are near to the o-b, and so the Side cannot affect the contact. If the angle is extremely wide, then we can apply running Side, taking care to get, at least, h-b contact. I may interpolate here that in forcing strokes h-b contact (with or without Side) achieves the widest throw-off. Forcing strokes, be it added, are not often needed by very good players, as they arise mainly from inaccurate positioning. Brute strength, by the way, is not the secret of forcing strokes, but freedom and accuracy of cueing, and it is necessary to avoid *less than*

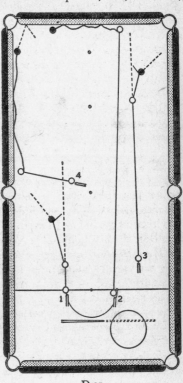

D.31

h-b contact. Top is very useful in run-through shots as it promotes extra forward rotation to the c-b which, owing to the essential thick contact in run-throughs, must, of course, lose some of its original forward rotation or speed. D.31 shows two strokes in which Top is employed. (1) When, in a run-through cannon, the c-b is near the first o-b, Top is necessary, for the reason just stated. So, in this stroke we use Top, with just less than full contact (naturally the point of contact being slightly to the left of full, as the red is to the left), and with a free-moving cue, run-through the first o-b to get on the second; a litttle check (r-h) Side may be used to keep the c-b from straying to the left, as shown here, but it is not indispensable; (2) a ricochet cannon, with Top and ¾-b contact, also strong r-h side, to strengthen the Top effect in keeping the c-b near the cushion in its wriggle towards the red; (3) here we do not use Top but low contact (Bottom) in cueing, as we do not wish to disturb the balls unduly, and the o-b is far away, so no force is needed: a slow stroke will result in a leave. In a stroke like this from hand (the "D") do not spot so as to make the stroke *less* of a run-through, but as full a run-through as possible, as here, i.e. (assuming this stroke were from hand) we would not spot to the right in such a run-through (No. 3), but at the angle the c-b lies (in the diagram). Almost full contact is needed; (4) this stroke is similar to No. 2, and is done the same way (i.e. with Top, l-h Side and ¾-b contact). Bottom should always be applied when we wish to slow up the pace of the c-b, as in Drag, for instance, but be careful not to convert it into Screw. Drag, of course, is Bottom (low) contact, but Bottom is not necessarily Drag. Drag may be called intensified Bottom, to preserve direction and Side effect, which, as we have seen, it delays. As a generalization, we might say the c-b should invariably be struck on the low side (with "Bottom") in slow- and medium-paced strokes.

Fine or Thin Strokes

By causing the c-b to make the thinnest of contacts with the o-b many an awkward situation may be surmounted, generally in positions in which the c-b and first o-b (in cannon play) are fairly near; if it is distant it is easy to make too fine a stroke. In fact, even in fairly close positions, the contact made even by good players is sometimes too thin. We have already seen some useful thin strokes in D.8. D.32 shows further ones. Stroke 1: A common position; we could pot red but would

have to send the c-b right round the table to get position, and
that would not be easy; by the fine stroke off red, which is
scarcely shifted, we retain perfect position. The way to make
such a stroke is to aim outside the o-b so that the edge of the c-b
skims or grazes its edge, or, to use the term generally employed,

play to "just to miss"
the o-b and then aim a
fraction nearer. We have
to make one edge skim
the other: it is useful,
in such strokes, to get
down very low. Most
players today play with
the cue near to, or ac-
tually scraping, the chin,
so there is not much
scope for a lower posi-
tion in their case, but
not all players adopt
fully the modern posi-
tion. When we shape up
for these thin strokes,
we should adapt our
stance, that is, alter it
from that for a h-b con-
tact, in other words,
make the direction of
our stance conform to
the line of aim.

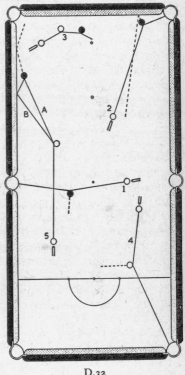

D.32

If the o-b is near a
cushion we play a fast
thin stroke to bring it
out, i.e. into play, as in Stroke 2. Stroke 3: A fine glancing
cannon, leaving possibly another or even two strokes of the
same kind, e.g. one back and then the same stroke again. The
majority of players do not quite realize the possibility of fine
strokes. Stroke 4, for instance, is a position in which most

players would play a $\frac{3}{4}$-b run-through, or would not attempt the loser at all, yet it is a practicable proposition. Stroke 5: Here we may make the cannon by *A*, a direct thin stroke, or *B*, a less thin, but still a thin, stroke, using the cushion. The cannon could be made by full contact on the object-white, sending it in and out of Baulk, but this entails the risk of sending it "safe" (i.e. out of play) or getting badly on to red. The thin stroke will send red over the pocket as shown. The advanced player executes these fine strokes, as it were, instinctively; a kind of knack, perhaps a case of knack or nothing, for even the best players often miscalculate, making the contact too thin or missing altogether. The possibilities of fine contact may be seen by placing the c-b on the r-h spot of the "D", the red on the Centre Spot, and trying to make a losing hazard into the *left* top-pkt—it can be done! A suggestion of optical illusion exists in fine stroke positions, as what appears to offer scarcely any scope for a fine stroke often, in the sequel, proves to have offered too much, for we make *too fine* a contact, and so miss!

The "Piqué" Stroke

I have dealt with Screw applied to the bottom of the c-b; in a position in which there is no room to apply orthodox

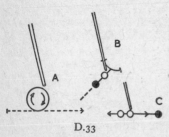

D.33

Screw (i.e. by low contact), we may apply it by the Piqué Stroke, that is, Screw applied to the top portion of the c-b. (See D.33, *A*.) As you will see, the cue is held vertically, the angle of its elevation depending on the degree of Screw we require. This Top effect promotes a slight run forward of the c-b, followed by fairly strong backward recoil. D.33, *B*, shows a Piqué loser, the c-b darting forward to contact the o-b, then, with the screw-back effect functioning, entering the pocket; *C* shows the same stroke for cannon purposes. The Piqué bridge is formed by tilting the hand, so that it rests on the table, supported, tripod fashion, by the three middle fingers, or in awkward cushion positions by the middle finger only. As stated, we use the Piqué Stroke only when there is no room to employ orthodox Screw or Screw back, either a cushion, a pocket or an o-b forming an obstacle.

In making the Piqué Stroke, provided you bear in mind that its object is to impart backward spin, you will not make the mistake of striking the o-b a "dead" thud, pushing into the table surface; the actual contact, which, of course, cannot be with the full tip-surface, consists of a sort of downward stab and the tip should, as it were, rather slide off the ball than dig into it. In practising, care should be taken to avoid striking the cloth, and a piece of thickish paper should be placed within an inch of the c-b, in case you miss the latter and hit the table.

The Piqué is really a kind of Massé Stroke, which I will speak of later, but it should be said straight away that only a handful of players, i.e. the professionals and a very few amateurs, can perform the Massé satisfactorily, and, as it is possible even to be amateur champion without playing a single Massé Stroke, the student has little cause to bother about such a highly specialized and difficult stroke, which some consider foreign to the English game.

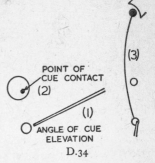

POINT OF CUE CONTACT (2)

(3)

(1)

ANGLE OF CUE ELEVATION

D.34

The "Swerve"

Generally speaking, the Swerve is more in demand in Snooker than in Billiards. Its object in both games is to evade an obstructing ball, as shown in D.34. The stroke is really downward, and vigorously, imparted Side. The bridge must be raised correspondingly, and, of course, be very firm. When-

ever Side is applied to the c-b a preliminary swerve effect
takes place, though scarcely perceptible. To secure a pronounced swerve, the cue must be tilted, and the stroke is,
as stated, tantamount to the application of strong Side with
an upraised or tilted cue. D.34 (1) shows the angle at which
the cue-butt is tilted; the extent will depend on the degree of
Swerve which is necessary; the higher the butt is raised, the
greater will be the degree of Swerve; 2 indicates the point of
contact; the stroke, as I say, is really putting on Side with the

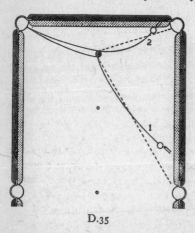

D.35

cue at a downward
angle, and should con-
sist of a kind of sharp
dig; the point of con-
tact, as shown, is a little
lower than that for or-
dinary Side. No. 3 shows
the purpose of Swerve,
as stated, and in the
stroke shown we can, by
Swerve, pot the red by
swerving round the in-
tervening ball; D.35
gives two interesting
Swerve Strokes. In each
of these two strokes the
in-off is narrower than the h-b loser, indicated by the broken
line in each case. Stroke 1: By raising the cue and contacting
the c-b on its r-h side, aiming to just miss the red, the loser
can be made; in stroke 2 we aim to just miss the red on its
near side, using r-h Side. In each case this results in h-b
contact. The other way to perform stroke 1, and the one
generally adopted, is by a fast fine shot, and, stroke 2, by
(a) a medium-paced stroke with extreme running (r-h) Side,
or a strong forcing stroke, with extreme r-h Side, sending
red round the table; it depends on how far away from the h-b
line (broken line) the red lies. If but an inch or so off the line,
a slow stroke with fullish contact on red, and the maximum

of running Side serves. I give the "swerve" way of doing these two strokes merely to illustrate the possibilities of Swerve.

THE BAULK AREA AND ITS SIGNIFICANCE

As we saw on p. 6, the area between the bottom cushion and the "Baulk-line" is called "Baulk". The two bottom pockets are known as the "Baulk pockets". When the c-b has entered a pocket as the result of a losing hazard, the player plays his next stroke from hand (i.e. the "D"), and he must play *out of* the Baulk area. He may place the c-b anywhere in the "D" space, including the semi-circular line and the part of the Baulk-line which forms the straight part of the "D". If he places his ball on this line (i.e. the straight line of the "D") then it must be exactly *on* it, which means half in and half out. If an object-ball is so situated, when a player is "in hand" (that is, playing from hand after having (1) made a losing hazard, or (2) retrieved his own ball from the pocket after the opponent has potted it during the latter's break), then that ball cannot be played on by the player in hand: such a ball is called a "line" ball (i.e. half in and half out of Baulk). A player, in hand, wishing to contact an o-b which is in Baulk must play *out of* Baulk to do so, and he can do this by a direct stroke (a screw-back), if practicable, off the other o-b if it lies out of Baulk, or by playing off it on to a cushion or cushions (out of or in Baulk). Or he can play directly off a cushion or cushions out of Baulk to contact the o-b lying in Baulk, say, to pot a ball lying on the brink of a Baulk pocket, or to make a cannon, if both o-b's are in Baulk. (See also Rules of Billiards, No. 4).

This Baulk area plays a major part in defensive tactics. If no score seems possible, or probable, we may pot the white (our opponent's ball) and send our own ball and the red into Baulk; or, if one o-b is already in the Baulk area (red), we may pot white and send our ball (the c-b) into Baulk to join it; or we may pot white and send one ball (i.e. red or the c-b) into Baulk. If we send both the object-balls into Baulk (or make one join the other) we leave a double-baulk; if we send one into Baulk, i.e. either the c-b or the red, leaving the other out (for we shall have potted object white), we have made a single-baulk.

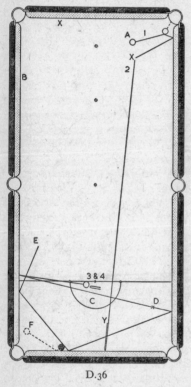

D.36

To score off a double-baulk is not easy, for both object-balls are "safe", that is, having to play out of Baulk, we cannot contact them directly. Thus the Baulk area is an important part of safety or defensive play. Look at D.36: red is lying against the bottom cushion, and is not well placed for scoring purposes; we cannot go in-off white, so we pot it (stroke 1), and (stroke 2) send the c-b into Baulk, to rebound to Y off the bottom cushion (in sending the c-b into Baulk for a miss from a distance it is always best to play off one or more cushions, as the direct stroke to the spot at which we wish to place it demands perfect strength, whereas cushion contact admits of some margin or error in this respect). Now, when making a double- or single-baulk, it should be our aim to leave ourselves a scoring stroke so that if our opponent, playing from hand (i.e.

out of Baulk), fails to score or disturb the two object-balls they may still occupy the position we left them in, i.e. a scoring one. Here, by going to Y, we have left ourselves a run-through loser off red. After our stroke to Y, our opponent may give a miss out of Baulk, say, to B, or he may, by a stroke off the side cushion (with l-h side) (No. 3), send his ball to D, so that, if we make our loser, the object white will be in Baulk, and, therefore, unplayable; or he may try to score by (a) a stroke off the top cushion at X, to contact the cushioned red on its r-h side, and thence to Y, or (b) play the stroke off the cushion (No. 3) but not, this time, to leave his ball "safe" (as at D), but (stroke 4) to cannon, if he can, off the side cushion, or, at least, destroy our scoring leave. As we see, he fails to score but partially succeeds in disturbing the position, contacting red, but, as its new position (F) still leaves a loser, and an easier one at that, he has failed to retaliate to our double-baulk effectively, and we have gained by it. We thus make the loser; and as his ball has travelled out of Baulk (to E) we are perfectly placed for a break. If he had left his ball at D, or at C, by a miss (a stroke which contacts no ball) we could probably have scored by a screw-back cannon (from Y, our position) if he left his ball at C, or a cannon off the side cushion if he left it at D.

Thus, by this tactic of potting the white (i.e. our opponent's ball), we secure a substantial advantage. In ordinary friendly play "potting the white" is seldom done. For some unexplained reason it has always been considered "unsportsmanlike" (for long it was called "Whitechapel", why nobody seems to know), but today in all serious play (championships, tournaments, club competitions, etc.) it is always done, and in any case all serious players have *always* ridiculed *not* "potting the white" when strategy requires it, and not to do so, even in friendly play, is to eliminate one of the attractive features of the game, viz. the duel of wits involved in defensive tactics, which, of course, are really offensive in purpose.

In D.36 we saw what is meant by a double-baulk when it is achieved by sending one ball to join another ball already in

Baulk. Often, however, we can get a double-baulk by sending the c-b and o-b there in one stroke, if we have lost the white or potted it and the red is not in scoring position. D.37 shows two double-baulks. (1) We send red and the c-b into Baulk by

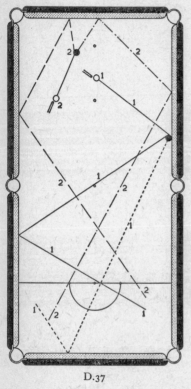

contacting the former on its near side, with strong r-h side to take the c-b into Baulk as well, and we achieve what we should always try to achieve (often it is not possible) to leave the two balls (c-b and o-b) at opposite sides of the Baulk area for a loser or pot. (2) By the stroke shown we do likewise, using l-h side to carry the c-b well round the corner to leave it on the r-h side, and suitably contacting the red to do the same with that ball, on the other side. In case (1) we have left ourselves a loser, in case (2) a pot or a thin loser.

One must be careful about giving misses. There is a rule which forbids a player to make two misses (i.e. a stroke which does not contact an o-b) in succession without a scoring stroke by the opponent in between them.* If, therefore, the red is badly placed, as in D.38 (stroke 1), and our opponent sends his

D.37

* A second miss can be made, however, if the player is faced with a double-baulk.

ball (the c-b) into Baulk, all we have to do to thwart him is to send the c-b into a pocket, 1B (called "running a coup"), for which we concede 3 points but gain a great advantage, for, in accordance with the rule referred to, he cannot give another miss, as our "coup" is not counted as a scoring stroke (it forfeits points instead), so he must now play on the red and, as it is so badly placed, the probability is that he will mull the shot and leave us something good. "Running a coup" is excellent tactics and is constantly a feature of the game. To guard, to the extent possibly, against this retaliatory stroke (the coup) we should, if possible, when giving a miss, try to place our ball in such a position (in relation to the red) as will, if our opponent runs a coup, give us a chance of scoring off the red. He will then think twice about his coup. In D.38, stroke 1,

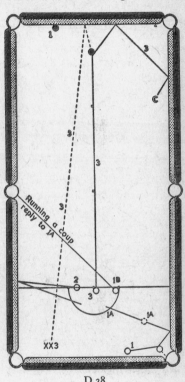

D.38

player "A" has potted the white, and then (1A) sent his ball (dotted) to 1A, inside the "D". Player "B" runs a coup, stroke 1B, so "A" must now play at the red (on top cushion). You see, therefore, the advantage of (a) running a coup, if our opponent will thereby be compelled to play at an awkward red; (b) anticipating the coup, by placing the c-b for a possible score (or Baulk stroke) off the red.

Start of the Game

The old way of opening the game was to give a miss off the side cushion to the "D", a stroke made with l-h side (D.38, stroke 2); the opponent might then give a miss, sending *his* ball against the cushion near a mid-pkt; the first player would then try to cannon off the red and two cushions. This opening is rarely played by good players now, as the opening miss invites retaliation in the shape of a coup (see above), thus forcing the first player to play at the red, a stroke which may go wrong. The opening stroke now, therefore, is that shown (No. 3) in D.38, namely, playing on the red, sending it into Baulk to stop near the l-h or r-h pocket (in the case shown, at $XX3$), and directing the c-b to the side of the table, to, say, C. The reply generally is to attempt the cannon from white (at C) on to red (at $XX3$). If it is missed the opening player has the red to play at, from C, for a loser or pot. Playing at the red, on its spot, from hand is always fraught with some risk, as, if we contact it badly, we leave it and the c-b in the upper half of the table for our opponent, but invariably the player succeeds in sending it into Baulk, as shown. Should he send it near the pocket, the cannon is often made (by the opponent), as it is easier to contact near the pocket. As playing at the red involves a risk, as I have said, it may seem strange that it has become the orthodox opening stroke, but, as a miss, such as the formerly used opening (No. 2), invites running a coup by the opponent there is no alternative, for if we do not play at the red at first we can be compelled to do so afterwards by the coup. (See also Rules of Billiards, No. 9.)

Defensive Play

Defensive play in Billiards and Snooker is called "safety play" but that is a misnomer, for defence enters into all games, and defensive "tactics" is a better term. The need for defensive play comes about when, say, having compiled a break we run into bad position and are faced with a stroke which we are likely to miss, and so leave the balls on for our opponent. Or our opponent may leave us a bad position, either when he breaks down or as the result of a "safety" stroke. Melbourne Inman, a famous "safety" or (as I prefer to call it) defensive player, used sometimes actually to bring his break voluntarily to an end, when he had lost position, and make a defensive stroke. This, however, more often than not consisted of potting his opponent's ball, and leaving him a double-baulk. It is very difficult to depict positions on a Billiard diagram wherein scoring would be difficult, given the hugeness of the actual table in comparison with a small diagram, and, as a matter of fact, even on the table itself no matter how you place the balls a score seems possible and, to a good stroke-player, probable. I give, however, on D.39 (1 and 2), two examples of the type of stroke which belongs to defensive play. The c-b (1) is, as

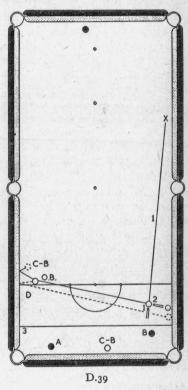

D.39

shown, near the r-h side cushion, the object white near the opposite cushion, the red near the top cushion. A cannon is "on", either off the r-h side of the red (thin) with strong l-h side, also off the white and side cushion, with r-h side, but in both cases more likely to be missed. If we send the c-b to X, we place it for a red loser, should our opponent run a coup; this stroke prevents his doing so. Or we may play at the white to change positions with it as shown (stroke 2). We could, of course, attempt to score, but if the position is critical, then some such move is often advisable, instead of going out for the doubtful score, and perhaps leaving our opponent an excellent break opening.

It often happens that our opponent leaves us a double-baulk which offers him the chance of a pot of, or loser off, red if we fail to disturb his double-baulk. Most good players make a safety miss to some other part of the table and let him make his pot, as he cannot easily get position from it, but in the case of the loser, such players generally try to disturb the balls, to deprive him of the chance which, if taken, must give him perfect position. D.39, No. 3, shows *A*, the red, and the c-b, in position for a pot in a double-baulk situation; if the pot is made, position must be doubtful when the red is spotted; *B* depicts the red placed for a loser in a double-baulk position: it is obvious that, with the loser made, and the red out of baulk, our opponent will be perfectly placed. The good player, however, in such a position often places his ball, after being the victim of such a double-baulk, *in Baulk*, but not in cannon position, say at *D*, so that, although our opponent is pretty certain to make his losing hazard, he will still have to rescue the white (our ball) from Baulk.

Attacking a Double-baulk

As I have said, when faced with a double-baulk one may (*a*) seek to destroy the position left by the opponent through his double-baulk, if it is a scoring position; or (*b*) make a counter stroke, i.e. a miss. By studying the angles of the table we are enabled to spot the c-b in a position whereby there is a fair chance of a cannon; this is the third alternative, when confronted with a double-baulk. D.40 shows three double-baulk positions, and cannons made by the opposing player. These cannons to score off a double-baulk position are always highly speculative, and, if the state of the game is tight, the better policy is to make a (defensive) miss, or to try to disturb the balls. No. 1 (D.40) is an up-and-down-the-table stroke without Side; No. 2 sends the c-b round the table (dead centre contact), effecting the cannon, as shown; No. 3: this is, as you will recognize, similar to the opening safety miss (see D.38)

but here it is not a miss but an attempt to score, and, as shown, it succeeds. As before, slight l-h side is used to effect the return off the cushion into Baulk. Here, the cannons are depicted as successful, but in the majority of cases, such attempts fail. Needless to say, there are countless such all-round or cross cannons, by which we may "attack" a double-baulk; these, however, will show the principle involved.

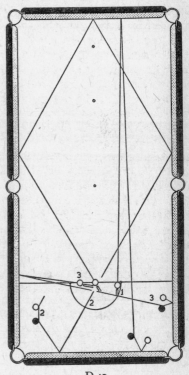

D.40

Naturally, good defensive play must be studied and cannot be improvised, as it were. It should not, however, be overdone as the ultra-cautious player fails in the chief purpose of the game, which is to score points. Nevertheless, in an important game, it is folly to play a wholly attacking game against a strong opponent, particularly if he is skilled in "closing up the game" (using defensive tactics) when the situation demands it. In defensive play, as in the game generally, the vital principle applies, that is, *never to make a purpose-*

less stroke. The main need is to study all phases of the game (watching the best players is invaluable) in order to be ready to employ strategical means as dictated by the state of the game and the calibre of the opponent. As I have said, the Baulk area is the main vantage-ground of defensive strategy.

SOME BASIC LOSING HAZARDS

Jennies, Long and Short

When the o-b comes to rest at, or near, the positions shown in strokes 1, 2, 3 and 4 (D.41) (i.e. fairly near a cushion), the result, of course, of an indifferent positional stroke previously, we play a stroke called the "Jenny". Strokes 1 and 2 are "Short Jennies". Stroke 1 is of very frequent occurrence. Place the c-b at the h-b angle, not for the centre of the pocket, but for the *farther jaw* (to avoid the near one); aim h-b and contact will be slightly fuller than h-b, and this you ensure by using strong check (here l-h) Side: the c-b will curl round with the Side into the pocket; if we played a pure, i.e. without Side, h-b stroke to the pocket opening, we should probably strike the far shoulder. Strike the c-b fairly low. We are playing into a rather "blind" (i.e. not fully open) pocket. If playing this stroke on the r-h side of the table, we must use r-h side (still check). The ideal Jenny of this kind should leave the o-b in the centre (if played gently) but most players by playing too strongly generally leave a Jenny on the other side, which is not advisable; you must try to leave the o-b in the middle. No. 2 stroke is also a Short Jenny, but with the o-b near the Baulk-line; a danger exists of sending it into Baulk, with the Jenny; to avoid this, the stroke must be made a kind of run-through, and you must, therefore, make a quite thick contact on the o-b. If, when practising this stroke, you find the o-b going into Baulk, it means you are not contacting the o-b fully enough, that is, probably, shirking the run-through, which, however, is the secret of the stroke. Spot for h-b, therefore, use a lot of Side, and thus ensure achieving $\frac{3}{4}$-b contact. Jenny No. 3 is a

Long one, and the two most frequent forms of this occur with
(a) the o-b below the mid-pkt, stroke 3; and above, stroke 4.
No. 3: Spot for a good h-b contact, and aim h-b, using, again,
plenty of check (here 1-h) Side—it is also pocket Side, as if
the c-b strikes the far-
ther jaw of the top-pkt,
the Side will carry it
into the pocket—and a
little over medium pace.
The o-b will probably
travel across the table
and come away from the
cushion into the centre;
a very slow stroke, to
bring the o-b into the
centre, is quite difficult
except for the advanced
player, but even he will
often use pace for the
stroke. If the stroke is
made slowly, then the
o-b will stop in the
centre of the table for
a loser. You will learn
to gauge your strength
in such strokes. No. 4
is a "Long Jenny"
with the o-b above
the mid-pkt. As it is
farther off, Drag serves
well with this stroke,

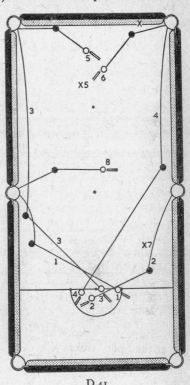

D.41

to preserve the Side as the c-b has farther to run. This
stroke is more difficult than No. 3, as the angle is less
inviting. In all Jennies, long or short, correct spotting is
essential, and h-b aim (and spotting) with Side will achieve
the correct contact. Jennies are of great variety, but all other
positions can be gauged from these four. When the o-b (white)

lies well out from the cushion, say, at X (stroke 7), the only stroke to make (leaving the other o-b out of account) is a loser into the top-pkt: this needs less Side and can be made at medium pace: spot for h-b, and use a little pocket (r-h) Side. As the pocket is fairly open, the c-b may enter it directly. In all Jennies follow through with the cue.

Run-through Losing Hazards

Perhaps no stroke is more mishandled, and missed, than the type of run-through loser shown in strokes 5 and 6. No. 5 shows the o-b touching the cushion: to run-through it, apply plenty of pocket Side (r-h here)—remember pocket Side means the side which will carry the c-b into the pocket if the opposite shoulder be struck (see p. 56)—play with a flowing rhythm, with follow-through of the cue, and contact the o-b almost full, i.e. a trifle on its side opposite to the cushion. Do not play a fast stroke, but one which brings the o-b just to the centre of the table ($X5$). A little Top is permissible in such a stroke, but it can be done quite well without, but, if Top is used, cue-contact on the c-b should be just a little above its centre (but don't forget the Side!). Play a medium-strength stroke, *not* a fast one. O-b, as stated, should stop in the region of $X5$, which should be your test of strength. Stroke 6 is the same type of run-through, but with the o-b *away* from the cushion. Where to contact the o-b in this stroke puzzles the average player. If, however, he will imagine the line connecting the centres of the c-b and o-b to extend to the cushion (at X), it will be clear that by correspondingly altering contact on the o-b (that is, slightly to the right of that imaginary extension) the c-b will accordingly "pass through" the o-b to the pocket. In short, instead of aiming to contact the o-b full, he will contact it a little to the right of full in accordance with the advice given previously. Owing to the o-b being in the open, the contact must be a shade less full than when it is touching the cushion. In all such run-throughs play a free, flowing stroke. Stroke 8 is a plain run-through, no Side, contact less than full in proportion to the difference between the point on the cushion, which the o-b would strike if contacted full, and the pocket.

More Important Losing Hazards—I

D.42: (1) *A vital stroke*; with the red placed as shown, a h-b stroke (1*A*) will send red to the side of the table (see broken lines (1*A*)); spot as shown (i.e. wide); use strong running (l-h) Side, contact red a fullish h-b, and play a fast stroke, the object being to bring red *round the table into the middle* (a thickish ¾-b stroke, with check (r-h) Side, thick contact to bring the red back as straight as possible off the cushion, might leave another loser, but there is quite a risk of sending it out of loser range); the h-b running Side stroke is the correct means. A shot essential to master. (2) Here, a h-b contact will send red in the direction of the arrow, i.e. "safe", or out of scoring range; so contact ¾-b to direct the o-b to *A*, and it

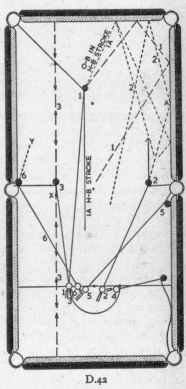

D.42

will come out into the middle off the top cushion; a *very important stroke*. As you see, by these two strokes, we must always try to keep the o-b in the loser area. Both strokes are vital in break-making. (3) A screw loser into the mid-pkt:

the point here is to make the stroke a *square* one, in order to send the o-b *straight* up and down the table (arrowed line), to stop on the straight line, and at *X* or thereabouts, if possible. An alternative method is to spot near the r-h spot of the "D", and try to drive the red on to the cushion early (as in stroke 2), after which it will travel round four or five cushions and perhaps stop favourably in the loser area; the loser is easier this way but the first way is preferable. (4) A screw loser into the Baulk pocket: use strong pocket (l-h) Side, contact red ¾-b (i.e. on its pocket side) and use strong Screw, but beware of imparting screw-back effect. (5) Red is lodged against the cushion an inch or so from the pocket: the thinnest of fine or glancing strokes, spotting where shown, and at fair pace, will score here. (6) Red is lying against the farther shoulder: contact it a little fuller than h-b, and at *slow* pace; the aim is to bring it slowly out into the centre, a too-thin contact will send it to *Y*, and a fast stroke will send it across the table (i.e. "safe" or out of loser range in both cases).

More Important Losing Hazards—II

D.43: (1) A screw loser, calling for plenty of Screw and ¾-b contact. A general rule for screw losers is that when the pocket is fairly open (i.e. when the jaws do not threaten to obstruct) running Side should be used; when it is blind, as here, check (here r-h) Side. If the player is capable of gentle, soft screwing powers, red, in this loser, will not travel into Baulk as the stroke can be done with ru ing Side and ¼-b contact, but the Screw effect would have to be very neatly executed. Thin contact would, of course, be less liable to send the o-b a distance. A clumsy, heavy shot will send it into Baulk. (2) A screw-back loser off red, with the balls in line: use powerful Screw and pocket (l-h) Side as the c-b may strike the lower shoulder. (3) A run-through through two o-b's: hit red full, as though sending the c-b direct into the pocket; red will strike white, and both o-b's thus clear out of the path of the c-b as shown; this stroke can also be done when the two o-b's are on the cushion (see 3*B*). (4) When the o-b (here the red) is placed as shown, a h-b stroke will send it off the top-cushion, then probably towards the l-h cushion; aim, therefore, h-b, with check (l-h) Side; this will result in a $\frac{3}{4}$-b

contact, and a thickish run-through (loser), the full contact bringing the red off the top-cushion fairly straight so that it remains in the loser area. (5) A similar run-through loser to No. 5 (D.41), but at a distance and rarely used: contact red full, with pocket (r-h) Side, fair pace. (6) A screw loser, with pocket (l-h) Side, fairly full h-b contact on red. (7) A run-through loser *against* the nap, use *r-h side*, for this reason, and the c-b will curve to the left, $\frac{3}{4}$-b contact. (8) The same stroke, $\frac{3}{4}$-b contact, *with* the nap, so that we use running (l-h) Side, the c-b curling, with the nap, into the pocket (the stroke may also be made plain

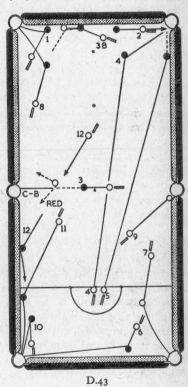

D.43

ball). (9) Object white against the lower shoulder: contact white $\frac{3}{4}$-b on the r-h side, with pocket (r-h) Side—in case the c-b strikes the lower jaw—and the c-b runs through the white, slow stroke. (10) A screw-back loser (as the c-b moves fast and, therefore, cannot be affected by the nap, no heed need be taken of the latter): contact a shade less than full, owing to the recoil needed not being quite straight, use strong (r-h) Side (i.e. pocket), as the c-b may strike the lower jaw; when such screw-back losers are into a quite open pocket, no Side is necessary, but in this stroke there is a risk of the c-b's striking the shoulder, as stated. (11 and 12) Run-throughs at fast pace into a Baulk pocket: use check (r-h) Side, as in No. 11, where the o-b does not lie far from the pocket; running (here l-h) when it does, as in No. 12.

Losing Hazards off the White

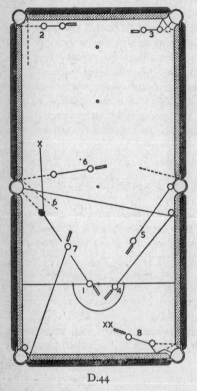

D.44

D.44: No. 1 is not "off the white", but shows how to *rescue the white* when it is in Baulk. We bring the red to potting position, as shown, by losing hazards, and then, before potting it, walk round to the mid-pkt area to ascertain the angle needed for the loser off white to bring it out of Baulk; in the diagram we presume the o-b (white) to be at XX, so, in potting the red, we aim to leave the c-b at X, thus leaving a h-b loser off the white and bringing it into play. (2) Using the pocket jaw to clear the object white from the pocket so that the c-b may enter (pocket (r-h) Side needed). (3) Dainty squeeze in-off, thin on white, r-h Side to give the c-b life, the c-b kissing the object white as that ball comes off the cushion, gentle stroke. (4) A chancy loser, but worth trying if nothing else is "on" and we are well ahead, Side (l-h) may be needed if the o-b is lower down the cushion. (5) White is on the edge, we contact a shade to the right of its centre by a slow-paced stroke with some r-h Side; the o-b getting clear off the jaw. (6) Another case of using the jaw, this time in a run-through losing hazard, object white escapes off the jaw, as shown. (7) Contacting the cushion first with strong running (r-h) Side, the c-b enters the pocket off the object white. (8) A kiss or squeeze in-off, made with thin contact and running (l-h) Side, to come smartly off the cushion. Even when the o-b seems to allow no space for the c-b to pass, a kiss or squeeze in-off is often possible.

VARIETIES OF CANNON PLAY

I have previously explained the significance of cannon play, and in this section will elaborate the theme a little and give examples of some important positional cannons. As I have said, calculated contact on both the o-b's is important; correct contact on one is indispensable for good Billiards. But even if we cannot make the desired contact on both balls, we must not forget the position of the ball we cannot control as we would wish when making our next stroke. The h-b angle figures prominently in cannon play, and, as in losing hazard strokes, we use it, or modify and calculate from it, as necessary.

The Drop Cannon

Perhaps the most important cannon is the "Drop Cannon", so called because the first o-b joins or drops on the other two prettily as the stroke is consummated. In the chief position or form of it, the red is on its spot and the white well this side of midway between the Billiards Spot and the Centre Spot and about 15 in. from the side (see D.45, *A*); this position may, of course, vary. The vital considerations in making this stroke are: (1) to contact the second o-b (here, the red) on the same side as the c-b approaches it (in D.45, stroke *A*, the r-h or "inner" side); (2) to contact the first o-b a fullish h-b; (3)

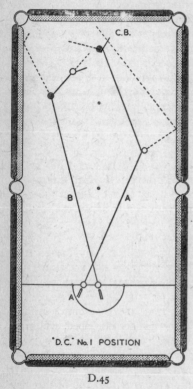

to employ the right strength, which should be medium. Stroke *A* represents this, the model example of the d-c. Some players, including the writer, employ a little check (r-h) Side, and contact the white a little thicker than h-b, a kind of run-through, the object being to make sure of contacting the red on the correct side, and this method also seems to produce good results, but the first-mentioned method is the authentic one. The reason why the red must be contacted on its inner side, as stated, is, of course, that it is the only way of directing it towards the pocket; contacting it on the

D.45

outer side or full would not achieve this, but would put it on the top cushion.

It must be emphasized that fifty d-c's will almost certainly produce fifty different results, and even the best player could not foretell to a nicety the positions of the balls after the cannon, and sometimes the after-position may be quite unfavourable, but provided the stroke is correctly played, excellent position is fairly sure to be left for close play, Top-of-the-table play or, at worst, a losing hazard. The d-c is one of the chief ways of "getting to the top" with a view to Top-of-the-table play. The stroke is a most fascinating one, enjoyable to make and to watch, and also attractive, in view of its slight uncertainty of outcome. In other words, it has at once the charm of the unknown and the promise of a lucrative reward. The good player, therefore, is always seeking to leave d-c position. Stroke *B* is an off-shoot of the orthodox d-c, and the same principle of sending the red pocketwards and the white towards the Spot applies; Drag may be used with advantage in such strokes. D-c's are akin to "gathering" cannons, as in many instances they cluster ("gather") the balls within a small area.

Contacting the second o-b accurately in the d-c is not so easy, and the stroke should be practised regularly till the c-b drops nicely on the second o-b, as desired, and at the right strength. The c-b is spotted, as stated, to secure the required contact on the red (D.45, *A*, No. 1 position) to direct it pocketwards. If, in the d-c, we wish to contact it finer or thicker for any special reason we must vary the spotting position accordingly, that is, spotting for h-b, to secure contact a shade more to the right (thinner), spotting should be that particular bit more to the left, and *vice versa*. Bad position may, and often does, result from the d-c, but, generally, accurate execution of it, in the manner described, will bring favourable possibilities, even if Top-of-the-table position is not favoured. When we come to the Top-of-the-table phase of the game, we shall perceive the significance of the d-c in that respect. Even if the player is not a Top-of-the-table exponent, as such, the d-c may lead to harvesting a nice little quota of points (two or three cannons and a couple of pots, for instance) until the cross loser takes us back to the "D" for the open game.

D.46 gives the second form of the d-c, in which the positions of red and white are transposed. In this form the actual cannon is also made by h-b contact, but the aim is to direct the white to the Spot or in front of it (as shown)—some call this "behind" the Spot—and to send the red off the cushion towards

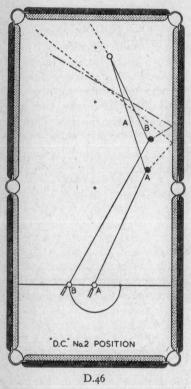

D.C. No. 2 POSITION

D.46

the opposite top-pkt. Should the red be higher up the table (stroke *B*) we may spot at *B*, or thereabouts, in order to get on the red in such a way as to direct it to the pocket (see the dot and dash line), and we use running (l-h) Side to make up for the wider angle, and thus get thicker than h-b contact, it being too high up the table for the pure h-b contact to give it the direction towards the pocket. These two positions, 1 and 2, of the d-c are the basic ones, but there are very many variants of the stroke. Nevertheless, in all of them, the aim is the same as in these two. Sometimes we do not succeed in either purpose, but find the three balls clustered together somewhere round about, or very near, the Spot, which again is a very satisfactory outcome, as after one or two little cannons we get the red in line for, or near, the pocket, and the white well situated near the Spot, for Top-of-the-table play.

Other Cannons

I cannot, of course, show more than a proportion of the vast number of cannons it is possible to make. I have selected some of the most important. Theoretically, a cannon is scoreable no matter where the balls are, but we are concerned with positional play, and if the three balls are, so to speak, all over the place, no good player, in a serious match, will do other than make a defensive stroke. All-round cannons depend on a good knowledge of the table angles, and are in most instances a speculation. D.47 shows two typical all-round cannons, which are worth playing, or not worth playing, according to the state of the game. No. 1 shows the white not far from the side cushion: in such a stroke, it is always better

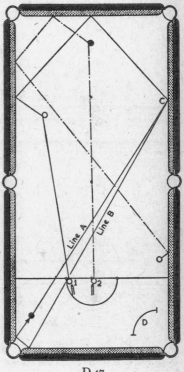

D.47

to play off the inner or cushion side than off the outer side of the o-b (all fear of a kiss is averted, for one thing). Here we use strong running (r-h) Side, to take the c-b well across the table to point C, the cannon being made, as shown. Should the c-b miss the o-b (red) directly, line A, there is a good chance of making the cannon off the bottom cushions, as line

B shows. No. 2 could be made by h-b contact if white were somewhere at *D*, but as it is higher up the table we must use some running (l-h) Side to achieve the sharper angle.

In cannon play a most important principle is to keep the

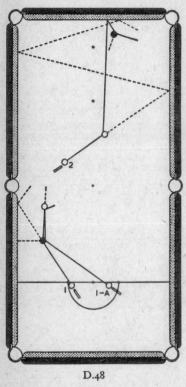

two o-b's in front of the c-b whenever possible. This often entails taking the first o-b thickly (a run-through), and the cushions help in such respect. The stroke in D.48, No. 1, illustrates the principle. By running through the red (1) we send it ahead (the right method); by spotting at 1*A*, to make the cannon more or less h-b, and easier, we send it to the side (as the line indicates) and it is left behind (a bad stroke). No. 2 is a similar and quite fascinating stroke: a h-b cannon would send white to the side cushion; by taking it almost full, thus directing it crossways to join the red, and using

D.48

strong check (r-h) Side to strike the red off the cushion, all three balls are brought together.

D.49: (1) A screw-back gathering stroke, sending red round the cushions, to return. As we saw (D.12), r-h side in such a stroke results in a l-h angle of departure from the cushion (the more Side we put on, the wider the angle). (2) A screw-back gathering cannon, bringing white back and sending the red towards the pocket; for the gauging of Screw effect, see p. 55. (3) A cannon, sending white towards the Spot, and red to the pocket, a basic aim in top-end play of whatever descrip-

tion. (4) A nice gathering cannon, using the cushions, fullish contact on red, to keep it straight, and running (r-h) Side to get a sharp rebound on to white, gentle stroke. (5) Slow cannon, with running (r-h) Side off red and the cushion, h-b stroke, medium pace, sending the two o-b's in the direction of the lines. (6) A run-through cannon off the cushion, after contacting red full, r-h side, to get on white, note the stroke keeps the o-b's in front of the c-b.

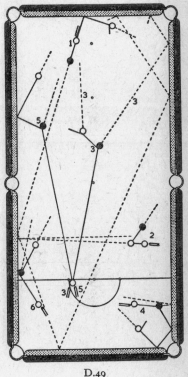

D.49

D.50: (1) A h-b stroke off the top cushion would score here, spotting between centre and l-h spots of the "D", but we should run the risk of potting white; to avoid this, spot at the *r-h spot* of the "D", use a little running (r-h) Side; this way has the advantage of bringing the two o-b's and c-b together, as shown. (2) A run-through gathering cannon, bringing white back off the top and side cushions; contact white almost full. (3) A run-through cannon, with some Top and some

Stun effect to get white out of the way and maintain forward rotation, after contact on white; use a little check (l-h) Side; c-b dribbles red to the pocket and white is sent out of Baulk. (4) An alternative though less used way of doing the cannon

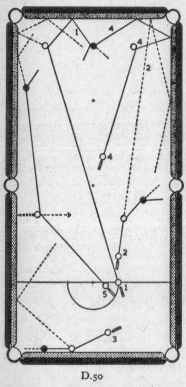

shown in stroke 1 (which could also be played from the "D"), h-b stroke: again the three balls come to rest together; most positional cannons need precise strength, and should never be made forcibly. (5) A h-b cannon sending red towards the pocket, and bringing white into the open; with the white and red positions reversed, we have to be careful not to pot the object white or place it in the pocket jaw; therefore in such a stroke we seek to contact it slightly on the l-h (cushion) side, also contacting red (now the first o-b) hard enough to send it to the opposite mid-pkt.

D.50

D.51: (1) Here we play a free stroke, contacting red at the point to send it off the cushion to the opposite pocket (i.e. fairly full), and, with strong running (l-h) Side, and are careful to contact white forcefully enough to send it near the Spot as the arrow indicates: the Side imparts an extra lively throw-off from red. (2) A nice gathering run-through cannon, ¾-b contact on red; this cannon places red for a run-through loser into the mid-pkt (stroke 2*A*), which returns red to somewhere near its original place; white is sent a little higher up the table. This alternate cannon and loser may sometimes be repeated three or four times, and was much exploited by the famous player, Willie Smith. Each time you make the cannon, of course, the white is sent farther away, and soon too far to repeat the stroke. (3) A cannon sending red towards the top-pkt, and getting on white for a mid-pkt loser, or cannon, according to position; this illustrates the principle of carrying an o-b up the table by thick contact. (4) By contacting white hard enough and with soft Screw, to send it just out of Baulk, we place red for a loser, thus rescuing both o-b's from Baulk, some l-h side helps to bring the c-b back. In strokes like 3 and 4, when we

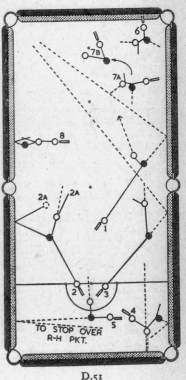

D.51

require to impart force to the first o-b, we play on it rather fully and a little forcefully, and the fullish contact takes the pace out of the c-b in Stun effect, as it were, so as to contact the second o-b gently. (5) A cannon which brings red back over the r-h bot-pkt, and sends white out of Baulk; some check (here l-h) Side, facilitating full contact, is useful in these gentle, square Screws. (6) A "squeeze" cannon, contacting each ball as thinly as possible, to get the correct side of the balls, "correct" meaning the side which enables us to use the top-pkts and area; the c-b in the diagram is, of course,

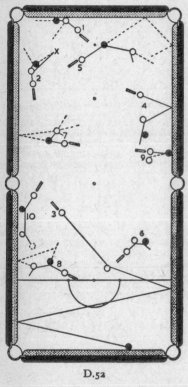

D.52

on the "wrong" side. (7A) A thin stroke across the face of red on to white, with a little running (r-h) Side to get clear of object white (a little running Side should always be used in these close-up thin contact strokes to avoid a "cover", i.e. the c-b's stopping too close to the second o-b); our object here, by this stroke, is to nudge the red forward, and get behind it for a Screw gathering cannon (7B), sending red into Baulk and back via the cushions (see stroke 1, D.49), as shown (7B). (8) A kiss cannon contacting white a little to the right, so that red comes off the cushion to meet the oncoming c-b.

D.52: (1) Here a fine cannon is not "on"; the only way to make the cannon is by a sort of quick Stun shot, despatching the white out of the way with a little running (l-h) Side to help the c-b on to the red, the forceful stroke clears the white away instantly, allowing the c-b to proceed. (2) A delicate kiss cannon, c-b and red meeting at X. (3) A cross-table cannon, no Side. (4) A cushion-first cannon; in this type of cannon it is useful to determine the cushion contact by making this half the distance between the c-b centre and the farther side of the first o-b, no Side. (5) A run-through cannon, slight check (l-h) Side, bring-ing the balls together by use of the cushions, and showing the value of thick contact on the first o-b, the check Side helping the thick im-pact. (6) A glancing cannon, with a little running (r-h) Side, al-ways useful in such strokes, in which the c-b contacts the second o-b slowly, to avoid the two latter finishing up touching or nearly so. (7) Another little Screw gathering cannon, with slight Side, using the cushion. (8) Again we make use of the cushion to gather the balls, thin contact on red permits full contact on white, giving thus enough pace to the latter to bring it well off the cushion. (9)

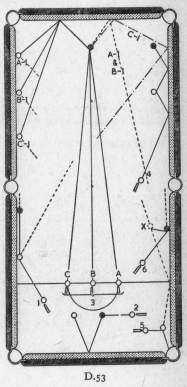

D.53

The "rocker" cannon, full rebound off red, skimming white; this stroke can sometimes be repeated a number of times. (10) The "pendulum" cannon sequence, consisting of successive glancing cannons; both 9 and 10 seldom crop up.

D.53: (1) A run-through cannon, full on white, with some l-h Side, to make c-b hug cushion. (2) This all-in-a-line position often occurs against the top cushion; a h-b cushion stroke will travel beyond the white; only a Screw stroke, off the cushion, also h-b, can score here. (3) Red on Spot, white in position A_1; spot at A, and a h-b fullish stroke

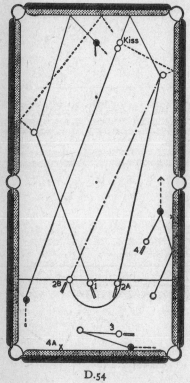

on red, sending it round two cushions into the middle, or towards the mid-pkt (broken line)—the thickness or otherwise of the contact will determine the course taken by the red—and making lively contact on white to bring it out from the cushion, will score. Fair pace is needed in these three strokes, otherwise red may be left awkwardly. A little Side may be used, in cannon A–A_1, as the angle is greater. Cannons B–B_1 and C–C_1 call for spotting at B and C respectively, as shown, and h-b contact likewise. (4) A cushion-first cannon: do not forget that the c-b strikes the cushion in advance of the point of aim so allowance must be made. (5) A screw loser, with thin contact, sends the white to X, and leaves a cannon (6) which the good player plays off red and the cushion, as shown; a gentle stroke leaves red over the pocket. To make the cannon off white direct is bad Billiards and does not ensure after-position.

D.54: (1) White is too near the cushion, i.e. outside the

h-b cannon; spot fairly wide and do the cannon off the top cushion, being careful to impart the direction shown to the white. (2) An important point is involved here, that is, avoiding the kiss, which takes place as shown if spotting at 2*A*;

spot then at 2*B*, with running (l-h) Side, and thinner than h-b contact; one must always be alive to the possibility of a kiss in this type of stroke; the remedy is, as shown, to spot differently. (3) A screw-back stroke, sending white out of Baulk and driving red to the pocket: always try to send the white out in such positions, placing red for a loser or pot. (4) A screwback stroke, with a bit of running (r-h) Side to come off the cushion smartly, red should be contacted so that it returns off the top cushion; if the white were at 4*AX* we should also do a screw-back stroke with running Side, as here, but would strike the side cushion at the spot marked.

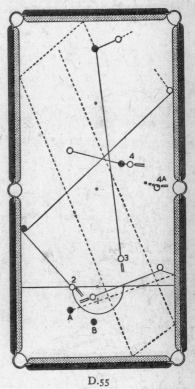

D.55

D.55: (1) Always a rather "tricky" cannon: with the o-b at *A*, we contact the white h-b, without Side; when it is farther down, say at *B*, we shall require a little running Side; this stroke will repay practice with the o-b placed at different angles; the tendency of the c-b to rebound fairly straight off the cushion is the snag, and must be allowed for. (2) By hitting the red and cushion simultaneously, and imparting all possible running (r-h) Side, it is possible to make the c-b take a very wide angle, as shown. No. 3 is a gathering cannon, which can

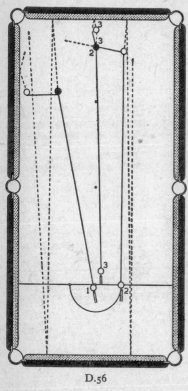

be made by spotting on the centre Spot of the "D" and bringing the red *straight* down the table and up again (strength to stay at the top), but this method involves the risk of its rebounding off the top cushion and straying too far from the top area. By making the red travel diagonally (i.e. round the cushions, as shown) the pace is retarded by the several cushion contacts and the red stays near the top: the stroke is shown out of Baulk, but it generally occurs with the c-b in hand, and the latter should be spotted at the angle shown (r-h spot of "D"). The red should be struck $\frac{3}{4}$-b, and the c-b partially stunned, so that it just nudges the white. (4) A run-through cannon with the c-b on top of the o-b: play a free follow-on stroke, hitting the c-b so as to make the cue-tip glance off the top (see 4A); this prevents our "pushing" (a foul stroke).

D.56 illustrates two common types of forcing or deep Screw cannons. (1) We cause the red to travel the length of the table

D.56

twice, taking care to strike it a little to the left of centre to give it the required direction, and we try to contact object white on its near side to carry it up, and not down, the table; strong Screw is necessary, no Side. A similar stroke is No. 2; here we must aim at contacting object white as full as possible, to avoid the risk of sending it near the r-h bot-pk⸱, and we must also contact red correctly to direct it towards the pocket, slight check (r-h) Side (l-h Side would risk missing red on its near side), strong Screw. (3) We often find the two o-b's situated as shown, i.e. one behind the other, when we are playing from hand; we place our ball (the stroke is presumed to be from the "D") on a spot a shade to the left or right (as here) of a straight line connecting all three balls, and then aim at red's centre; the red will kiss the white on to the

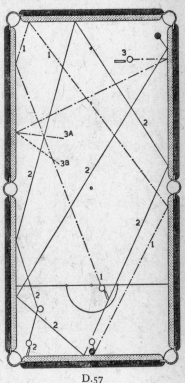

D.57

cushion, and owing to the fact that we are a shade off the straight line, will kiss the c-b as the latter advances. The paradox of this stroke is that we must make a slightly faulty contact on the red to score as, if we spot absolutely straight, and contact the red dead full, the c-b cannot get by. Use Bottom for this stroke.

D.57 gives (1) a key stroke for getting to the centre of the

bottom cushion by a round-the-table stroke played from hand.
The point to contact is about five inches below the Spot (side
cushion), and running Side should be used. The stroke is
useful because, by varying the cushion contact, we may contact another spot on the
bottom cushion corres-
ponding to the differ-
ence in the side-cushion
contact. The pocket
must be avoided in these
variations of contact.
No. 2 shows a six-
cushion cannon, with
$\frac{1}{4}$-b contact on white
and plenty of r-h side.
(3) A peculiarity of Side
is that running Side off
one side cushion
changes to check when it
contacts the other: the
stroke 3 shows this.
The c-b, with running
(r-h) Side, comes off the
opposite cushion with
check Side, in direction
$3A$; if the Side did not
change but remained
running Side, it would
take direction $3B$.

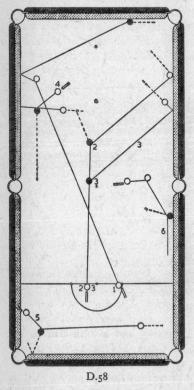

D.58

D.58: (1) A useful
cushion cannon, with
slight running (r-h) Side to contact red; more or less Side is
used according to the angle of the stroke. (2) White is touching
the cushion; cannoning off red, we must try to hit white fairly
full, avoiding getting behind it, as this may send it into the top-
pkt; by a slow stroke, and fairly full contact on its near side, we
bring it off the cushion, probably leaving a white loser. (3) A

similar cannon, but with white a trifle away from the cushion; here we must be careful to contact the cushion first to send white into the open; again care must be taken to avoid sending it towards the pocket, in which we may lose it. (4) A nice cannon off red on to the cushion, slight l-h side, to send it to the mid-pkt. (5) An important stroke; by very thin contact on red and a slow-paced stroke we aim to leave red for a pot, then, in potting the latter, to place the c-b for the in-off off white, thus rescuing both balls from the Baulk area. (6) Red is out of play; by extreme running (r-h) Side and gentle strength we cannon on to red, and dislodge it from the cushion, leaving probably a soft screw loser into the mid-pkt.

The large variety of cannons shown is, of course, but a small part of the countless ones that we may have to make, but the player who masters the selection featured will be able to meet most (cannon) requirements of the game, and, confronted with others, will have the requisite knowledge to apply them.

THE SPOT STROKE

There is no better practice for potting than the old Spot Stroke, of which the famous player, W. J. Peall, and his contemporaries were such outstanding exponents. The stroke was barred in 1898 because these players were scoring so prolifically by it that the game was becoming lopsided in the same way that it did later, in the 30's, when nursery cannons threatened to dominate it unduly, and a limit had to be imposed on them. Nevertheless, there are those who consider that the Spot Stroke, too, should merely have been limited, instead of being cut right out of the game, particularly in amateur play, in which it would make a pleasing additional ingredient.

The Spot Stroke consisted of potting the red ball into either of the two top-pkts until, of course, a pot was missed, the red being spotted after each pot. The object white did not enter into the matter. The fact that Peall, in 1885, executed a Spot

Stroke run of 634 pots would alone suggest that nothing is
easier than to keep potting the red, but besides potting, great
art lay in positioning the c-b after each pot, and, as we know,
positional play is the basis of Billiard (or Snooker) art, and is
not easy! D.59 shows the two areas within which the c-b must
be kept if a Spot Stroke break is to continue. It is obvious that,
as the c-b occupies but a pin-head's space in comparison with

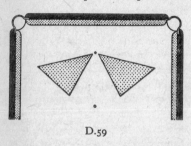

the huge area of the playing surface, countless
variations of contact and
angle will be possible so
far as potting the red is
concerned; these, how-
ever, are all related to the
few basic positions of
the Spot Stroke, which I
will give here. As the red

D.59

ball, after being twice potted from its spot, must be transferred
to the Centre Spot, unless one of the pots is made in conjunction with a cannon, when the rule does not apply, it is obvious
that the Spot Stroke sequence can no longer be played. Nevertheless, although obsolete, there is no more valuable form of
practice for potting, and also for the Top-of-the-table game,
two of the most important phases of the game. To play the
Top-of-the-table game well, one's potting standard must be
very high, and a missed pot, provided it forms part of the
Top-of-the-table sequence, should be a comparative rarity. If,
therefore, you can become proficient at the Spot Stroke, you
are well on the way to becoming a good Top-of-the-table
player, and your all-round or open game, not to mention other
phases of the game, must thereby improve out of all recognition. As differing degrees of strength are involved in Spot
Stroke technique, from fairly forceful to gentle, and as Stun,
Screw, Side and Follow-through are all part of it, the immense
value of proficiency at it needs no emphasizing.

Ds.60–66 feature the main strokes. The pot can be made, of
course, from countless other positions of the c-b (in the shaded

areas) than the ones shown, but the types of stroke they illustrate, that is, the plain pot, the stun pot, the screw pot, the
run-through pot, the screw-back pot form the means whereby
the red is potted, whatever the position, so long as the latter
lies within the two shaded areas shown in D.59. The pot can
still be made from outside them, but it is not easy to get
back into them from such a pot, and the smooth sequence
of Spot Strokes depends, for the most part, on the c-b's being
kept in these areas. The line *A—B* in Ds.60–66 is the straight
line to the pocket, permitting a straight screw-back pot, and
it provides a guide to the type of stroke needed when the c-b
wanders from it. If the c-b can be made to return straight
from contact with the red in the screw-back pot every time,
then, of course, quite a number of such pots can be made.
Memmott, an Australian professional of Spot Stroke days, was
stated to have made over 400 successive screw-back pots, and
Peall once made 184. Care should be taken not to screw back
too far from the red, the closer the better.

D.60: A gentle run-through, plain ball, c-b being just above
the line and a straight screw-back is not on. The run-through
takes the c-b to correct position on the line on the other side.

D.61: C-b just below the line; a screw-back stroke, placing
it back on the line by a nearly full contact; even if one cannot
screw back straight, i.e. on the line, the next pot may be made
by one of the other types of stroke shown.

D.62: A difficult stroke, which is an integral part of Top-of-
the-table play, and also of the red and Black sequence in
Snooker; a two-cushion run-through, with some Top, to
promote the run of the c-b; some running (r-h) Side helps to
bring the c-b well "round the corner"—it promotes a livelier
throw-off from the cushion than plain ball—and also reduces
the needful pace of the stroke, which should not be in any
way sluggish. The Side makes the pot harder, of course, but
one must learn to pot with Side, and this stroke is fine
practice for that, apart from its vital function in Top-of-the-
table play, and Black-and-red play in Snooker. The cue should
not be held rigidly, and the stroke should be free and flowing.

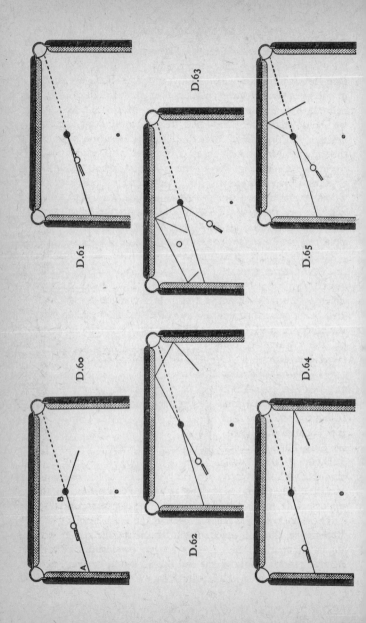

D.60

D.61

D.62

D.63

D.64

D.65

D.63: Position will determine here whether we should pot the red by a Screw Stroke (the round white shot), or a thick Run-through Stroke, with running or check Side, according to the need to get after-position near red: if the c-b were half-way between the *A—B* line and its position in the diagram, we should make the Screw pot, the c-b coming off the side cushion, as shown. With the c-b, as shown, however, we make the top cushion pot with check (r-h) Side. This Screw pot is the stroke to make, in Top-of-the-table play, when the object white is situated as shown. Screwing round it (see diagram) we get position for a cannon (white to red), the use of which will be seen when we deal with the Top-of-the-table game, for by it we can restore the object white to its place near the Spot and get on red in line for a pot.

D.64: If the c-b is farther away from the red than in D.60, but at the same angle to the pocket, the run-through, a free stroke, requires a little more strength, and the c-b should be taken to the far cushion, to return to a position on the line, this being safer than a stroke of calculated strength, to stay, as shown. A little running (r-h) Side may be needed to come off the cushion at the angle shown.

D.65: A rather strong run-through, stunning the c-b somewhat, and bringing it back off the top cushion as shown, no Side, but some Top.

D.66: A Stun run-through, with thick con-

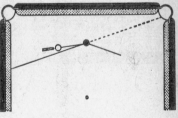

D.66

tact, the c-b slowly advancing to the line position on the opposite side, use a little Top, striking the c-b rather forcibly.

These then are the main strokes in the Spot Stroke game. Experience, through practice, will familiarize the reader with the positions from which to play the various strokes, and after regular practice, potting the red off the Spot, or from anywhere in the top area, will lose its terrors. Of much importance,

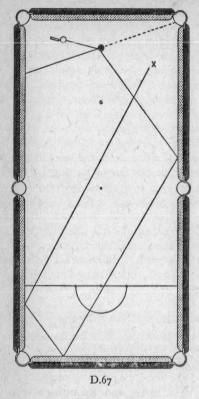

D.67

for progress in this stroke, is the *need to practise hard at each stroke* before attempting to see what size break you can make.

If the c-b comes as high up the table as in D.67, position is lost and can be regained only by a stroke, potting the red, and sending the c-b right round the table to finish at X, to come to rest in one of the areas of D.59. I repeat, the strokes shown are for the purpose of conveying the technical means of potting the red from the various angles; each type may itself vary, that is, to take one example, we may have to run through the red in various ways, according to the position. Each stroke shown represents the principle of that particular type of pot. It is for the player to vary the particular type, as necessary.

TOP-OF-THE-TABLE PLAY

The chief advantage of the Top-of-the-table game, which consists of pot-and-cannon sequences, and is a derivative from the Spot Stroke, is the reduced field of operations it offers, for, instead of the whole table, as in the open or all-round game, being required, a mere eighth of its space, at its top end, save for an occasional stroke or two, suffices. By virtue of this reduction of space, the player has the three balls confined within an area which forms about an eighth part of the table; in other words, he is close on top of them all the time, and in the words of a famous amateur player, "You only have to tickle them along"!

Paradoxically, however, Top-of-the-table play is an art at which few amateurs excel, for, offsetting the advantage mentioned, is the fact that it bristles with pitfalls. For one thing, it demands ability to pot the red ball from all sorts of angles, as in the Spot Stroke, with at least 90 per cent. success, and failure to do so means presenting one's opponent with an ideal leave (i.e. red over the pocket, with the white handy). Moreover, cannon play in this type of game has to be of a highly skilled and delicate order, and it is easy to get into trouble. This top-end game demands, furthermore, a delicate touch and command of strength, an advanced degree of proficiency in ball-control, and, of course, precision of positional play.

The top-end game is, apart from Nursery Cannon play, the most remunerative form of Billiards, and points can be scored there much more rapidly than at the open game, or the predominantly losing hazard game and, moreover, it requires much less travelling round the table, the player having only to walk from side to side of it, at its top end. Requiring a very large amount of regular practice, and being, as stated, considerably more difficult than other modes of play, it may be asked why the average amateur need bother about it. The answer is that if the serious student aims at becoming the "compleat Billiard player", with designs on the highest honours, he cannot afford, and certainly if he is, as he must necessarily be, a true artist, he cannot remain content, to ignore such a profitable and fascinating branch of the game, and if he devotes time regularly to practice, and possesses real ability, it is most probable that he will master this game reasonably well, and he will assuredly get great pleasure from it.

There is a further reason, and a very important one, why he, and every player who is trying to rise above the ruck, should aim at Top-of-the-table proficiency, and it is this. In Spot-end play it is possible to score quite a number of points before taking the risk which will leave the opponent ideally placed, should the stroke be missed. That is, having made these points, the player, instead of taking such a risk, returns to the open game by creating an opening for a losing hazard (the cross loser), to get back to the "D". This limited exploitation of the top-end game makes a very valuable reinforcement to the all-round game, and, skilfully interwoven into it, increases considerably a player's scoring potentialities.

It rests with the student himself, however, what will be his objective, that is, to become what is known as a "Top-of-the-table player", namely, one who regards this mode of play as his main objective and scoring force, or to incorporate it, to a partial extent, into his general game, as I have just suggested. If, of course, a player finds his touch and style do not lend themselves to the Spot-end game, then, of course, he will confine himself to the open game. Nevertheless, even an all-round player should familiarize himself with the moves in the top area, for they crop up unexpectedly in any type of play, and any serious player should know how to deal with such positions to the best advantage, if only to avoid pitfalls. The true aspirant, however, to mastery of an art will not place limits to his progress, and my advice to any player aiming at proficiency, is to study and practise top-end play even though he may feel it is not for him in competitive play. Let us now take a look at the strokes and tactics of this mode of scoring.

D.68 shows the ideal position for Top-of-the-table play, though the object white need not necessarily be against the cushion. Provided it is lying between the Spot and cushion, the position is all one could wish for. The cushion position, however, lends itself to what is termed the "Postman's Knock" stroke, so called from the "rat-tat" which ensues when the c-b, after contact with red, in the cannon shown, strikes the object white a second time after the latter's rebound from the cushion. The red is taken, when perfectly placed, h-b, but, as the c-b's position may differ a little, slightly thinner or thicker than h-b contacts on the red may be necessary. Consequently, the path of the red towards the pocket, from the cannon, may be *A*, the most common, or *B*, also very frequent, or *C*, which, however, does not occur in this position except once in a while. Which of *A* and *B* ensues will depend on the angle of the cannon, but if the position is that of the No. 1 "ideal" position (D.68), then *A* will invariably follow. If the cannon by a slight variation in the position

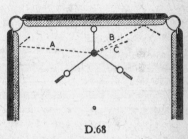

D.68

(D.68) should require our sending the red, as in *C* direction, we must take care not to use too much strength, as, if we do, we may pot the red prematurely and thus destroy position. If the o-b is against the cushion, as shown, we may be able to continue the "postman's knock" sequence, i.e. first the cannon, as shown, then the pot to bring the c-b back to the same position, for quite a number of times, until the white is shifted. Robert Marshall, of Australia, three times world amateur champion has often scored 60 or 70 points by this stroke. If, of course, we get straight on the red, we may, before making the cannon, get in an extra pot by the screw-back stroke, securing, thereby, an extra 3 points. Nevertheless, as stated, you need not worry about dislodging the object white from the cushion, for, provided it remains in the vicinity of the Spot (even on the other side of it—see D.83), you can continue playing Top-of-the-table. In all phases of this type of play, the aim, immediate or eventual, is to place the red for a top-pkt pot and the white in proximity to the Billiard Spot, the c-b being steered to either cannon or potting position. Naturally, keeping the three balls in the requisite relationship over a period is not easy, but extensive study and practice will develop control, and generally, when position is lost, or likely to be lost, the player can, by leaving a losing hazard when making his pot or cannon, return to hand.

The object white will constantly evince a tendency to stray from the Spot area, and confining it there is the player's constant care. Sometimes, to keep it there, we shall have to play a sequence of close cannons, i.e. cannons at close range, *not* nursery cannons (see p. 128). Dismiss any idea you may have that Top-of-the-table play is a kind of strict formula, demanding mechanically precise positioning of the balls in every stroke; it is a fluid process and allows a certain latitude in the course taken by the balls. Strictly speaking, of course, the movements should approach, as much as possible, to a set pattern but, so long as the pot and cannon objective is adhered to, we can stay at the top.

In the "postman's knock" position (D.68), we aim to pin the white there for as long as possible, but if it strays, provided we keep it round about the Spot, all is well. As we must nearly always, except, for example, when screwing off or stunning the red, or running-through it, to pot it, play at as gentle a pace as possible at the top, we shall find that whenever we are a little out in position, a cannon or two (or more) will suffice to restore position. It will serve to familiarize the reader with the moves at the top if I illustrate a few of the strokes which are common to Spot-end play. These are not, of course, the only ones possible, for, as I have said, it is not a matter of machine-like motions in set grooves. A first-class player's sequence, may, and does, with the accuracy at his command, develop a *comparatively* stereotyped pattern, but, even in his case, minute variations of contact call for variation in treatment.

It must be emphasized that as there are three balls involved, and, therefore, three after-positions from each stroke, in Top-of-the-table play, it follows that the number of possible types of stroke in a Top-of-the-table break are countless, and, consequently, such a break cannot be made by rule-of-thumb, as it were. When, however, the student has acquired knowledge of the main principles of such play, and begun to familiarize himself with the off-shoots from the basic strokes, he will acquire an instinctive ability to "navigate" the waters and shoals of this most fascinating branch of the game.

D.69: Here object white is a little to the left; we contact it on the right, with slight r-h side, to avoid a cover. It must be our constant endeavour to avoid the latter for it invariably means an end to the Spot-end game. By a cover is meant, of course, leaving the object white in between the c-b and the red (D.73). Contact on white should be thin to prevent the latter straying from the Spot area, red is sent towards the pocket, gently. D.70: Red is potted h-b to leave the cannon. D.71: Cannon off the top cushion, with some l-h side, very gentle stroke, rather full on red so as to take pace out of c-b, to reach object white slowly, red, of course, passes object white before c-b contacts the latter. D.72: In potting the red (D.71) we seek to leave the c-b as in D.71A, with a view to knocking object white back to its "ideal" position in the ensuing cannon; as the diagram shows, we contact object white very thinly and drop gently on red, no Side. D.72: A similar stroke to D.71, with l-h side, with the object white nearer the centre; this top-cushion stroke is all-important and the reader must bear in mind that in this type of cannon the object white must never be struck on the same side as the c-b is lying; that is, we may strike it as in Ds.68 (dead centre or thereabouts), 71, 72 and 76 (from behind) or D.74 (on its far side) but seldom, as in D.89 (i.e. on its near side—this diagram shows the bad results of so doing, as the subsequent pot red is covered or obstructed by the intervening object white). D.73: Another splendid position for Top-of-the-table play; we contact red a nice h-b, and nudge object white at its centre; if the latter is rather near to the red, then we may have to partially run-through red in order not to get the wrong side of white, and some r-h side will thus be useful; remember, we must always beware of a "cover"; D.73 (side of diagram) illustrates such a mishap from striking white on its wrong side in this and other positions. D.74: If we *must* contact white on its *near* side, we should apply strong running (l-h) Side to make a quick getaway of the c-b from white and cushion; a run-through cannon, however, may be possible, as the diagram depicts; D.75: As we cannot drop on object white centrally, owing to the c-b's straight position, we use running (l-h) Side to come well away from

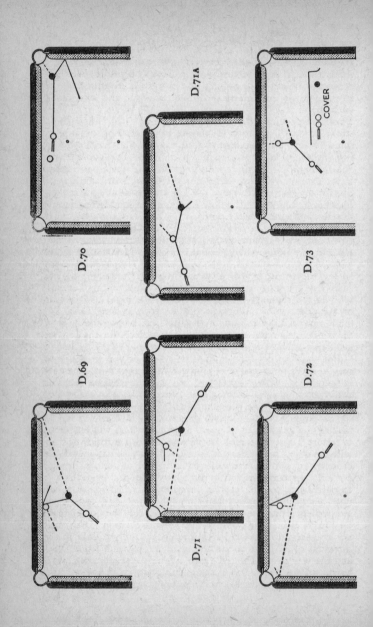

D.69

D.70

D.71

D.71A

D.72

D.73

COVER

the cushion and to avoid a cover, taking care to contact white very thinly, slow pace, so as to move it as little as possible; even ¾-b contact on object white might result in a cover. D.76: Stroke 1: running gently through the red while potting it, and leaving the cushion cannon (2) with l-h side from the other side. D.77: Stroke 1: potting red, with slight running (l-h) Side, gentle stroke, to get the position (as shown) for the cannon, made with some l-h side, which places red for the pot, and sends white a few inches to its appointed position. D.78: The two-cushion run-through pot we dealt with in treating of the Spot Stroke. D.79: Cannon restoring white to its position, with check (r-h) Side, to make the narrow angle, and Bottom to stop c-b straying. D.80: A variant of D.73, with o-b's close to each other; we run-through red rather thickly, with a little check (r-h) Side to ensure getting centrally on object white, to nudge it away from the c-b, so that no cover ensues: sending the white cushionwards in such a position is always the game. D.81: Cannon contacting object white very thinly indeed, with slight running (l-h) Side, to make sure of not missing red, an awkward position, as striking red thickly will destroy position (a screw-back gathering cannon, sending red round the table, might be made here, but we may try the stroke shown, as it does not destroy position). D.82: We might make a direct cannon on to white here, but we should send the white away from the Spot; by playing off the cushion we avoid this and keep it in the vicinity, as shown. D.83: The second "ideal" position for Top-of-the-table play; in this position we seek to make the gentlest of contacts on object white, so as not to move it more than necessary, and to nudge red on to a line with the pocket, for potting; it is often possible to make four or five cannons in this position before the object white is driven too far away to continue; when that stage is reached, we, in making the last pot, try to leave a cannon which will enable us to restore Top-of-the-table position, and No. 1 position at that, with the object white situated as in Ds. 68 or 73. D.86 shows this cannon; in potting the red, stroke 1, by a follow-through pot off two cushions, with some r-h side, we send the c-b to position 2, for the cannon in question, which, as you will note, sends the object white behind the Spot, and pushes the red pocketwards. If we strike red on its r-h side the position will be equally good. Note that in this second position (D.83) it is not necessary to send red near the pocket, only a little in the direction of it. D.84 shows the resultant position from D.83, and the way to pot the red (with perhaps a shade of r-h side) by the stroke which leaves the position shown in D.85. D.87: Two gathering cannons, No. 1: running through object white

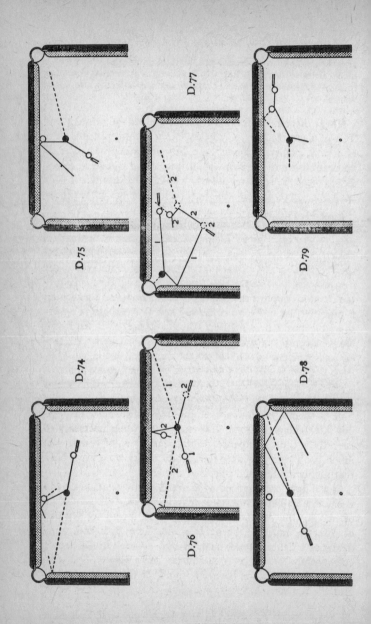

D.74

D.75

D.76

D.77

D.78

D.79

and directing it to its proper position, while dropping on red to direct it towards the pocket; No. 2: sending red across the table to stop over the near pocket, and directing object white spot-wards.

These diagrams will initiate the reader into the principles of Top-of-the-table play. Countless positions are possible and, of course, cannot be shown here, but, as stated, the reader, if he bears in mind the main objectives of the Spot-end game, viz. to place the red for a pot when making the cannon, and to keep the white around the Spot, will have no difficulty in cultivating this fascinating branch of the game. I have not illustrated the screw-back pot, always to be made when possible (for an extra 3 points), because its place in the scheme of things is obvious; that is, whenever we are straight behind the red for a pot, we make our 3 extra points and leave the c-b where it was. In the first "ideal" position (D.68 or D.73) the cushion prevents the object white straying, and by keeping it more or less in between the red and the cushion, Top-of-the-table position is assured. In this phase of Billiards we must be careful to use minimum strength whenever we can, and always try to get well on top of the balls, that is, we must keep the c-b as near to the o-b's as possible, in a manner of speaking, caressing them, the cue being a sort of magic wand. A little Bottom stays the pace of the c-b, when necessary, and Side is used to avoid the cover, and to gain position; the stun pot is an integral stroke, and enables us when necessary to keep the c-b on a sixpence, so to speak. It is, of course, not much good worrying over the second position until we have thoroughly studied and practised the first.

It will have been noticed by the reader how valuable the top cushion is in Top-of-the-table play, and always the advantage of making the cannon off it (D.72 and D.76, 2), instead of directly, must be borne in mind. The Spot-end game demands a delicate touch and, in fact, all the refinements of cuemanship the player can muster. The expert Spot-end player keeps the white hovering round the Spot, and manœu-vres the red for the pot by judicious cannoning. It is often

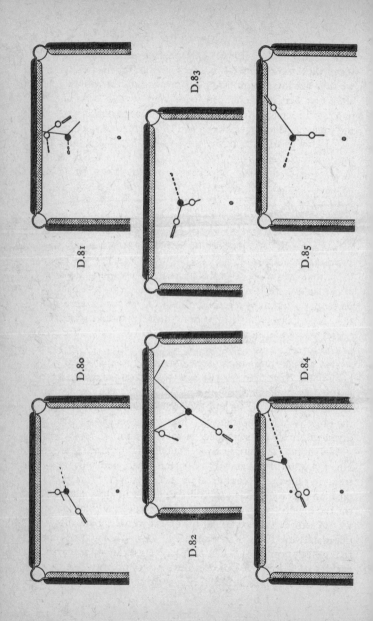

D.80

D.81

D.82

D.83

D.84

D.85

unnecessary to place it near the pocket from the cannon, provided we can place the c-b in good position for the pot. Often we may get in an extra cannon or two, when the o-b's are all close together. If we happen to get the "wrong" side of the two o-b's in such a (close) position, we manœuvre them for the squeeze cannon (see D.51); and thus return to the "right" side, i.e. the Baulk side, of the o.b.'s. Not only the top, but also the side cushion(s), may be used to restore position, as in D.87. Top-of-the-table play calls for the application of all forms of cue compensation (that is, Side, Stun, Drag, Top, Bottom, etc.).

I said that often one may make two or three cannons running in Spot-end play, and, of course, if you are a nursery cannon player you will designedly try to get the position on the top cushion for a sequence, but the ordinary player is not likely to be that (as yet, at any rate!). Often by foreseeing the next stroke or two, we can, at the top, get the object white back to its proper position by a second cannon. D.90 is an example of this. Most players in this position (stroke 1) would graze the object white and gently send the red to the pocket for the pot. But, seeing the white is not ideally placed, we make a second cannon, skimming the red, and directing the white to behind the Spot, and by our cannon we have restored ideal position and still have the red placed for the pot. As I said, we should always be on the lookout for a chance to restore the object white to position if it has strayed. The two strokes involved are shown separately in the diagram.

We should, of course, always endeavour to keep position No. 1 (Ds. 68 or 73) and get back to it when we have strayed from it, unless, of course, it is easier to get to work on position 2, D.83, which needs, be it said, ideal touch. Although the red may lie handy for the pot, do not pot it, if by a cannon we can remedy the position of the object white, should that be unsatisfactory. D.88 is an example of this. We could pot the red in both positions, but in each case the cannon, as shown, enables us to improve object white's position. After this cannon we can then pot the red. A final word of advice! The good

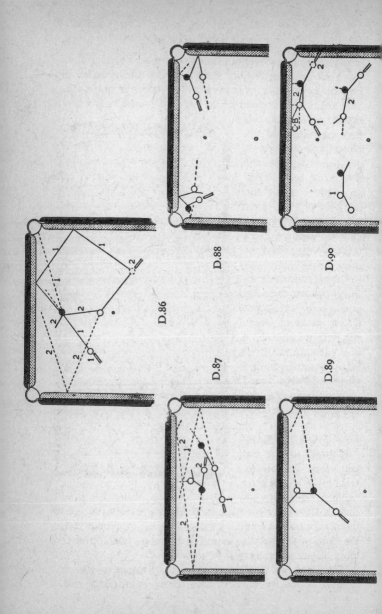

D.88

D.90

D.86

D.87

D.89

Top-of-the-table player does not worry about "coming away" (by a losing hazard) from the top, when the situation has become awkward, for, as we shall see later, getting back is very simple, the method being: (*a*) by a losing hazard into a top-pkt, to send the o-b into position for the Drop Cannon, or (*b*) to pot the red and leave the cross loser (D.6, 4), which sends the red over a mid-pkt. If it does not finish favourably for a pot red, we must by one, two or more losing hazards into that mid-pkt, try to bring the red over the pocket for the pot (D.92, stroke 2) which will enable us to return to the top. In this cross loser, contacting the red a trifle thinner will send it over the mid-pkt for the pot.

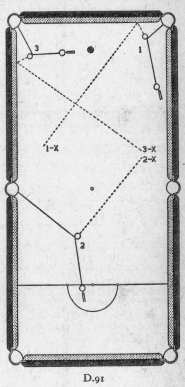

D.91

How to get to the Top

Getting to the top end for Top-of-the-table play is not particularly difficult, although often quite good amateurs find the opportunity eludes them for a time, a fact due no doubt to that capricious factor, the "run of the balls". Generally, however, the Top-of-the-table player experiences little difficulty.

There are two chief ways, the first by means of the drop cannon, which, as we have seen, generally speaking, either bunches the balls together at the top, or sends the red towards a top-pkt, and the white to the Spot. D.91 shows three losing hazards, made with the purpose of leaving the o-b in d-c position, the red being on its spot. Stroke 1 is made with a

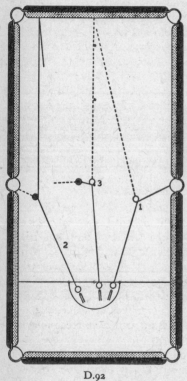

little finer than h-b contact and some running (r-h) Side (to compensate for the thin contact) to send white to $1X$; No. 2 is a thin loser, plain ball, sending the white to $2X$; No. 3 is a soft screw loser (thin) sending white to $3X$. From these three positions the d-c may be played. If one o-b is in d-c position, we, as in these strokes, make a losing hazard off the other (assuming it permits), to send it to occupy the position necessary to make the d-c. If it does not lead to that position first time, we may be able to make it do so by a second or third loser. If we cannot place the second o-b in position for a d-c we may be able to leave it for some other kind of cannon which will bring the balls to the top area. (See Cannons, D.49, 3, D.51, 1.) The other chief way of reaching the top is that shown in D.92. In this method we make a loser (No. 1) off the object white, whereby the latter is sent to the Spot area, and then (No. 2) pot the red in a mid-pkt, and in that stroke direct-

D.92

ing the c-b to position for the Top-of-the-table cannon when the red is spotted (No. 2). It is best to make the c-b rebound off the top cushion, as shown, as reaching any given spot by this sort of stroke without the aid of a cushion rebound is none too easy. If the white and red are not adjacent to the mid-pkts, for so disposing them, as shown in the diagram, we make the necessary losing hazards off them with a view to bringing them into such positions. The choice between these two methods of acquiring Top-of-the-table position will depend, of course, on the run of the balls. No. 3: This position sometimes occurs, and leads to Top-of-the-table position, as shown. White is sent to the Spot, by a cannon, and, afterwards, red is potted and the c-b directed to Top-of-the-table cannon position off the side, or side and top cushions. We should take care to keep the c-b a little to this side of red, so that, in potting it, we may send the c-b to Top-of-the-table cannon position (D.68).

Final Remarks on Top-of-the-table Play

Although in many quarters amateurs are "warned off" from Top-of-the-table play, notably in books, such advice dates from the days when red-ball play was the "rage" and before top-grade amateurs had developed the skill at Spot-end play they have long since acquired. Any student of the game worth his salt, will, I am sure, feel a challenge in such an attitude, and make it his firm resolve to attain a reasonable degree of mastery at this most fascinating branch of the game, be it only to incorporate it (to the partial extent I have recommended) into the all-round or open game.

It is reasonable to suppose that if the foremost amateur Snooker players have attained such a remarkable degree of skill in potting, as exists today, Billiard players can do like-wise, and, if that is so, the most serious obstacle to success at Top-of-the-table play will have disappeared. By practising the Spot Stroke, potting the red from all angles will be mastered quite sufficiently to "play Top-of-the-table", assuming, of course, that the player has a natural aptitude for skilled Billiards in general. It is a great pity that the custom has long prevailed of having tables in public halls and in clubs, etc., of which the pockets are larger than standard, as it results in amateurs being able to make reasonably sized breaks at the top, with such pockets, only to find that when they come to play on standard tables, such as are used in championship play, etc., they come to grief, finding the standard pockets difficult after the "easy" pockets referred to. Every table should conform to the official type but, as things are, the fact that proprietors of halls and clubs do not wish to make the game difficult for their patrons, and that for obvious reasons, stands in the way. No serious-minded player will, however, want to play on an "easy" table, but, unfortunately, the vast majority are not serious-minded and wish only to enjoy themselves and not to make good progress. The serious-minded player should, therefore, always steer clear of tables with over-size pockets and, fortunately, many clubs and halls, where the game is taken seriously, endeavour to provide one table, at least, with standard pockets.

Summing up, the player should, in Top-of-the-table play, aim at cultivating delicacy of touch, and thus acquire facility in keeping the c-b as close to the two o-b's as possible, thus making the different strokes as "easy" as possible. A great variety of contacts are involved in this phase of the game and, therefore, all manner of contacts should be practised, from the thick run-through to very fine. Whenever it is possible to get in an extra pot red, the opportunity should be taken, as it means 3 extra points, and this, of course, requires that the screw-back and stun pots be mastered. After you have potted the red and it is placed on its spot, provided you have left the c-b more or less in a line with the pocket, you are able to make the screw-back pot, and remain in position for your cannon. If, however, the red is slightly off the pocket line, and it is, therefore, hard to get cannon position, do not hesitate to leave the cross loser, and never try to retain top-end position if it is awkward to do so, but leave the cross loser. Skill at making close cannons, that is, from positions in which the three balls are all near each other, will enable you to regain the orthodox Top-of-the-table positions by one, two or three (or more) of these dainty strokes, leading to the little squeeze cannon (see D.51, 6) by which the

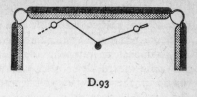

D.93

c-b may be transferred to the other side of the two o-b's and Spot-end position thus restored. Besides missing the pot red, another pitfall in Spot-end play is failing to secure accurate

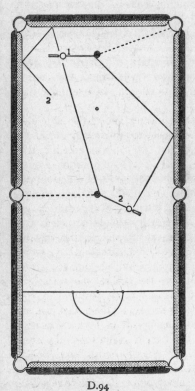

D.94

cannon position after potting the red and coming off a cushion or cushions with the c-b, with either too much or not enough strength (e.g. in the pot of D.78). Often check Side or Bottom, or both, have to be employed to prevent the c-b straying too far down the table and to "come off" the cushion at the required angle. Cushion contacts, therefore, should be frequently practised. A position worth consideration often occurs at the top; D.93 shows it. The object of this cannon, which provides a way out of the awkward situation, is to place the white for a losing hazard: by making the cannon off the cushion, this is done. Should the white be actually touching the cushion, by contacting it on its outer side we cause it to rebound off the cushion by the kiss effect, and it will permit the losing hazard. D.94 shows an interesting way of regaining Top-of-the-table position when, having potted the red once off its spot, we cannot do so again because it will have to be transferred to the Centre Spot. We *do* pot it again, however, and send the c-b to a position just below the Centre Spot, so that, when the red is spotted there, we may pot it, as shown, and regain cannon position, when it appears on its own spot again. The Rules require the amateur to cross the Baulk-line (with the c-b) once in every 400 points, and, to do this, those amateurs (very few) who are capable of making a break of such dimensions, play to pot red at an angle similar to that of D.94 (1), and in making the red pot, send the c-b down, and round, the table, so crossing the line and returning to Top-of-the-table position. Professionals must cross the line once in every 200 points.

THE ART OF BREAK-MAKING

It has often been said that the art of making breaks consists of leaving a succession of "easy" strokes. The celebrated John Roberts, the "W. G. Grace of Billiards", however, often declared, "there is no easy shot in Billiards". These statements appear quite opposed, but, when explained, are not so. Countless strokes are "easy" in themselves, but no stroke is easy taken in conjunction with positional requirements. In other words, it is often easy to score, but to leave the balls in good position for the next scoring stroke needs the elements of calculated touch and strength, the use of such things as Side, Bottom, Drag, etc., all of which convert the simplicity of the actual stroke into comparative complexity. Therefore, it is well to revise the opening remark and substitute: "The art of Billiards consists of leaving scoring position after each stroke". This art, of course, demands the ability to anticipate, and, therefore, the player must get into the habit of seeing a

move, or two, ahead. This is not easy, but, if cultivated, perfectly realizable. The gift of leaving a succession of scoring
strokes is, in other words, the art of ball control. Now, control
is quite impossible without mastery of strength and accuracy
of contact. I am assuming the player to have arrived at a
reasonably efficient stage of cueing and stroke mastery. When,
consequently, he has reached the point at which he should
study the art of break-making, it is advisable that he (in practice of it) play each stroke slowly and deliberately, so that
accuracy may be attained, and in order that he may cultivate
the art of choice of stroke. As he makes progress, and his
breaks increase (which will be the proof that he is making
headway), he will find his sense of position and anticipation
become more "instinctive", as it were.

This form of practice will at the same time develop what we
call the "Billiards sense", that is, the gift of sensing the correct
policy to pursue in each of the countless positional contingencies that arise. Ball control involves the command of
strength and also precision in contact. In the latter respect, a
good plan is to set up a h-b cannon position in the open, and
practise contacting the different contacts on the second o-b,
i.e. $\frac{1}{4}$-b, h-b, $\frac{3}{4}$-b, and the intermediate degrees of contact
(see D.3). Various other cannon positions can be set up with a
similar object, particularly the two d-c positions, that is,
(1) with the red on the Spot, and (2) with the white near the
Spot, and the red in the usual (basic) d-c position (see D.46, A).

A "stroke player" means one who, as the term implies, is
very good at executing strokes and does not concern himself
overmuch with positional play. Such players are hard to beat
in short games, especially if favoured by luck, but stand little
chance against a really good positional player. Positional play
belongs to the category of art which conceals art, and as the
result of it is to make the game look very easy, the average
spectator does not realize the skill involved, for it is more or
less hidden, as he does in spectacular stroke play. In a word,
the positional player, by manœuvring the balls accurately,
leaves strokes which, in themselves, are easier than those left

by the good stroke player, whose leaves are more often than not fortuitous. Thus, executing shots of a brilliant order elicits more applause from the uninitiated than the kind of stroke which forms a link in the chain of calculated strokes we call a break. It is, however, the art of positional play that the student should aim at since it multiplies scoring power so much the more. Positional play leads to good breaks; the good stroke player, by his disregard of position, may break down at any moment, and is continually encountering difficulties. The player who excels at ball control, foresees the next stroke, and the next, and has little need of luck. To put it succinctly, he is controlling the balls; in the stroke player's case, the balls are really controlling him.

Big breaks in themselves, however, are not the target, for a player often makes a high break in the course of a match and does not get near that figure again. What he does do, however, is to make good breaks consistently, and whenever the position of the balls favours a break he takes good toll of the opportunity. Every aspiring player, therefore, should do his utmost to cultivate the touch, control and foresight which enables him to place the balls accurately. A big break is very often not repeated in a session or match because the player's concentration, accuracy, mood, etc., have all coincided, in point of maximum expression, in that break, and he has probably been favoured by that good fortune which consists of all the little "accidents" of ball contact on cushions, pocket jaws, avoidance of a near kiss of the balls, etc., turning out in his favour, not to mention escaping the distractions that may come to a player's concentration in the shape of an audible remark, a sudden door banging, ill-timed applause, etc., all of which may cause a breakdown. We should not, therefore, look upon big breaks as necessarily the target, but rather the ability to score consistently from good openings. If the positional skill is there, breaks will flow from the player's cue.

There are, roughly speaking, three types of game to play:

(1) The "red-ball" game, in which the player scores mainly by losing hazards off the red, employing the cannon merely as

a means of recovering position for loser play, or for gaining position for it when a losing hazard is not on. Prior to 1926, consecutive hazards (losing and winning) were unlimited, and that was the day of the red-ball player, as such. In 1926 a rule was passed limiting consecutive hazards to 25, which is the limit today, except that in the Amateur Championship and some other important events the limit is 15. After 25 or 15, as the case may be, hazards, the player may continue his break only by making a cannon, or a cannon in conjunction with a hazard. This rule had the effect of reducing exploitation of the red, but a great many players, especially those of average ability, still make most of their points by red-ball play, hence the expression a "red-ball player".

(2) The "open" or "all-round" game, in which the losing hazard plays the principal role, but cannon play and modified Top-of-the-table play supplement the losing hazard, the player losing no opportunity of leaving a d-c, which, of course, takes him to the top area, where he indulges in a brief spell of Top-of-the-table or close play (cannons and pots, though not specifically top-end play), and then, by a losing hazard, returns to the open game; most good amateurs favour this type of play.

(3) The Top-of-the-table game, in which the player's object is to get to the top end, and there make all the points he can by this method of scoring.

The accomplished red-ball player is difficult to beat as, making the bulk of his points by losing hazards in the mid-pkts for as long as possible, and, when no longer possible, into the top, his score, at 3 points a stroke, mounts impressively. Most amateurs, however, do not, as stated, specialize in red-ball play today, and play a game (the open game) in which, although losing hazards are necessarily the mainstay of their play, cannons and visits to the top end, where a few pots and cannons are effected, enter into the scheme. In the open game there is, of course, no fixed course for play to take, since in countless positions more than one scoring stroke is possible, and one stroke may lead to a d-c and some top-end play, while another may lead to a bout of losers. The essential thing is that if we keep on making positional strokes, scoring opportunities will always follow, and while we make this or that stroke we must have the next one in mind. If the reader has never got beyond 30, 40 or 50, although he may have been playing for years, the reason, of course, is that he is not striving to leave one scoring stroke after another. Let him begin to take heed of this and his play will improve. He should say to himself, "I'm never going to make another stroke without thinking of where I am going to leave the balls." Let him not worry about missing or losing; the day may come when not only will he begin to beat those who now beat him, or become a worthy foe, but also when he will be making good breaks consistently.

We must always, when both o-b's are well placed, take both into consideration when making our stroke and visualize where both will be after our stroke. Billiards is a three-ball game, and the more this is kept in mind the more beneficial will be the result, and the greater the breaks made. If we decide that the red ball is our best hope, then we should study red-ball play in all its phases, noting the position of the red after every form of mid-pkt and top-pkt losing hazard, and, furthermore, we must always relate to our red-ball scoring the position of the object white, the function of which is to rescue the red whenever it has run safe from a bad stroke. In playing on the red, therefore, we should previously have taken care to leave the white in an advantageous place, if possible, permitting a losing hazard, or, at the worst, a cannon, should red position be spoilt. The majority of the best amateurs of today are, however, open or all-round players who exploit the red when the opportunity occurs, but also the d-c and similar openings for play, thus combining all three phases of the game, losers, pots and cannons. Provided we play with a consistently good touch and use all shades of strength judiciously, ball control will ensue and, with it, good breaks. The secret of good Billiards is "purposeful" stroke-making. As long ago as 1858, one Edward Mardon, in a book about Billiards, wrote: "Devote your leisure hours to practice" and "never strike the balls wantonly, nor without a precise object", and there you have it in a nutshell. The vast majority of Billiard players do so strike the balls, hence their failure to make good breaks. When they do make a break of 30, 40 or 50, which is perhaps once a year, it is by luck, not by judgement. I give now some main principles to observe in break-making:

(1) Break-making is, of course, not possible without the most important thing in Billiards, true cueing. One-ball practice, every time you take up a cue, will ensure this; if you cannot make the c-b return straight over the Spots, something is wrong with your stance, delivery, bridge, etc.

(2) The run of the o-b must be studied in practice and friendly games so that it is *always* taken into consideration.

(3) Never make a purposeless stroke, that is, one which scores but sends the o-b's anywhere.

(4) Always play the positional stroke in preference to the "scoring" stroke, however easy, which does not permit of position being left.

(5) Whenever possible, in cannon play, avoid separating the balls; and play the run-through cannon, if possible, to keep the two o-b's in front of the c-b; often this will not be possible, but more often it will; do not forget the invaluable aid of the cushions in "gathering" the balls together.

(6) Practise with the rest, and, if possible, with the left hand, which will make the use of the rest unnecessary in a great many instances.

(7) Do not try to get the required position (e.g. d-c position, Top-of-the-table position, etc.) in one stroke, unless, of course, it is practicable; play, if necessary, two or three strokes to get it.

(8) Make the d-c one of your chief objectives; it invariably places the balls favourably at the top end, and leaves a variety of openings. Even if you are not aiming to be a Top-of-the-table player, the d-c and its varieties (namely, cannons which gather the balls at the top) lead to a position in which quite a few points can be scored; after scoring a few, therefore, the policy of making a losing hazard and returning to hand is the one to pursue, and the points gathered in this fashion will materially add to your aggregate.

(9) When making a top-pkt loser, with the c-b near the top, make it so as to leave a cannon, should the other o-b be in favourable position for it.

(10) When the three balls are fairly close in the open, make sure you do not leave a "cover"; a little running Side helps to prevent the c-b remaining too close to the second o-b.

(11) Remember that if you reach the stage of making a 50-break by positional play you will have become a really good player, for a 100-break is two 50-breaks joined together, and a 200-break, four 50-breaks and so on. Therefore, when you

can make 50 by positional Billiards you may call yourself a true
Billiard player, but when you do reach this 50-break stage you
will find that you do not stop there; your breaks will grow
bigger and bigger.

(12) Gentle strength is the aim in most strokes, but not always.
Many strokes require a certain amount of force (Long losers,
gathering cannons, forcing strokes, etc.); but whenever we can
score by a gentle-paced stroke we must do so.

(13) The indifferent player concerns himself primarily with
the c-b; the average capable player, with the position of the c-b
and one o-b; the first-class player, with the position of all three
balls.

NURSERY CANNONS

Nursery cannons represent the most delicate branch of
Billiards, but as those amateurs able to execute them in match
play, that is, with a competent referee in charge, are very few
indeed, it follows that they are really outside the scope of this
book. You might attend the whole of the Competition Proper
in the Amateur Championship and not see a run of nurseries
worth the name. In 1954 R. C. Wright, of Hinckley, made a
run of 50 (100 points) in the Amateur Championship, but, as
stated, "nurseries" are rare, runs of half a dozen being
occasionally made by first-class amateurs, but the stroke is not
a feature of amateur play. In the 30's professionals such as
Walter Lindrum, Joe Davis, Tom Newman and Clark
McConachy made the nursery cannon such a monopolistic
feature of the game that measures had to be devised by the
ruling body for limiting it.

It may seem pointless, therefore, to devote any attention to
a stroke which does not figure in amateur play to any appreciable degree, but, just as the player who adopts the all-round
game may benefit considerably by making himself familiar
with and, indeed, practising seriously the Top-of-the-table
game, which, but partially exploited, as I have pointed out,
adds substantially to his scoring powers, so will a partial
study of, and also practice of, the nursery cannon enhance the

quality of touch and add to the skill of the aspiring amateur. If indeed such a player should find that he possesses the necessary touch and command of delicate strength for nurseries, then, of course, he will be in a position to consider whether he should incorporate it into his game. It is quite certain that if an amateur developed real skill at this stroke he would be a serious contender for world honours. Many amateurs are able to perform a sequence of nurseries in practice, but, as I have said, they are unable to do so in serious play when a referee is present and when each cannon must be legitimately made, the tendency being, in practice, to make many such cannons by the "Push" Stroke, which, of course, is a foul.

One difficulty in nursery cannon play is obtaining position for a sequence of nurseries and, in endeavouring to gain position, it is easy to sacrifice other scoring opportunities. The best place for a run of nurseries, that is, a series of cannons with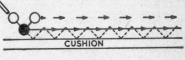

CUSHION

D.95

the three balls adjacent to a cushion, the latter, of course, serving to prevent the balls straying from position, is the top cushion. D.95 shows the main idea of the stroke. The first stroke is made on to the red, as shown, and the intention is to steer the object white along a straight line, and the red also along a line, but in zigzag fashion, as illustrated, each cannon leaving a similar one, in theory! Naturally, even the great nursery cannon player does not maintain pinpoint accuracy in so directing the two o-b's, but he does keep them in the same relationship, despite the great difficulty of preserving a uniform delicacy of touch throughout. No half-hearted stroke, in the fear of striking too hard, will succeed. I said the sequence was, in theory, one of similar strokes, but in practice the balls, even though departing but minutely from the ideal position, require countless different contacts and types of stroke, in which Side plays a formidable part. Ds.96 and 97 show some of the countless positions the balls may assume in a run. D.96: *A* needs a thin glancing stroke; B shows the red against the cushion, and, as it must be sent forward to catch up with the white, we impart some check (l-h) Side, which achieves this purpose. If we wish to hold the red back, when it is thus lying against the cushion, we apply running (r-h) Side. The explanation is that

D.96

when the c-b contacts the red, a kiss takes place and, at the second contact of c-b and o-b, the Side on the former produces the opposite Side on the latter (that is, check on the one ball produces running Side on the other). If we wish to *detain* the red, when against the cushion, B, we should use running Side (here r-h) which would result on check Side being imparted, by the kiss recoil, to the o-b, just as, in certain forms of mechanism, one cog-wheel causes another to rotate the opposite way. One or two believers in what is called "transmitted" Side instance this as a proof of this theory, which postulates that running Side imparted to the c-b can transmit the opposite Side to the o-b, but although in the present instance it is indeed a case of transmitted Side, the effect is wholly caused by the cushion. C shows a cushion-first cannon; D is the dreaded separation of the two o-b's, the c-b having got in between them, so that position is spoilt for further nurseries; E is a glancing stroke from the "outside"; F is the second pitfall, a cover, also destroying nursery position. D.97: In stroke A, l-h side is needed to come off red adequately, and stroke B is a kiss cannon.

D.97

Although nurseries are also called close cannons, there are, as we have seen when dealing with cannons, countless close cannon positions in the open which are not nurseries; nurseries are, generally speaking, those made with aid of the cushion. The great Australian player, Walter Lindrum, made the world's record for nurseries in 1933, when he took the balls two and a half times round the table, making 529 cannons (1,058 points). D.98 shows one way (there are others) of "turning the corner". Getting past the mid-pkt is still more tricky but we need not go into that here! D.98 (2) is an ideal practice stroke for achieving the sort of delicate touch needed for close cannon play. It consists of directing the c-b full on to the o-b (against the cushion) repeatedly, leaving the c-b in position each time as it rebounds. Another exercise for nurseries is to use the object white only and, with the c-b, try to direct it gently along the straight line shown in D.95, the c-b working from side to side; this can also be done by

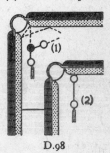

D.98

doing the same with the red separately, sending it against the cushion, to follow the zigzag pattern it should conform to (see D.95).

I conclude with some hints for acquiring nursery cannon touch:

(1) Change position for each cannon, i.e. feet and cue-alignment, except, of course, in positions permitting the same stance, etc.

(2) Make a decisive stroke, not a half-hearted prod.

(3) Hold the cue lightly, not tightly.

(4) Maintain a regular rhythm.

(5) Do not push the ball by placing the tip too near.

(6) Do not push the tip through the c-b when a cover occurs; if practising, play the stroke again.

(7) Vary the pace according to the stroke; there is no uniform pace for nurseries.

(8) Practise a series of close cannons in the open, to acquire the touch for nurseries.

(9) Do not check the cue-action; cultivate a "swing" or

rather "slide" of the cue; in other words, keep the cue moving.

(10) Practise each cannon slowly; do not try to emulate the expert nursery cannon player until reasonable proficiency has been attained.

(11) Concentrate particularly on the inside ball, positionally.

(12) Observe the effects of Side, Top, Bottom, etc.

(13) Reverting to the position when the red is touching the cushion, I advise you to place it there, with the c-b at the angle shown (D.96, *B*), and experiment by contacting it successively: (1) Centrally, (2) with l-h (check) Side and (3) with r-h (running) Side. This will teach you a lot.

(14) Use Side to avoid "touching", very little, of course.

(15) When you lose position, replace the balls; do not continue.

Needless to say, this does not pretend to be anything but a presentation of the main idea of the nursery cannon, a conception which any player should have, but which only the advanced player need trouble about seriously, and as you could win the World Championship without performing one sequence of nurseries, it follows that you will still be worthy of joining the amateur elect of Billiards if you cannot shine in the least at nurseries. But they facilitate delicacy of touch!

THE MASSÉ STROKE

The student need bother little about this stroke, the object of which is to make the c-b travel *round* an obstructing o-b, in order either to score a cannon, in which case it must, of course, skim the obstructing ball, or to score a loser by entering a pocket after evading the obstructing ball. The player holds his cue almost perpendicularly and raises his bridge which rests on two or three of the tilted finger-tips, a sort of tripod. The Piqué Stroke is a sort of screw-back, with the Screw applied to the top of the ball, instead of to the bottom; the Massé is

'Screw and Side" applied to the top, to produce curve or swerve. The c-b is pinched between cue and table; and the point of contact lies within the top surface area of the c-b, but varies according to the type of stroke. The reasons why the reader need not concern himself with the Massé are that but a handful of amateurs perform the stroke with any degree of success; that only a few professionals possess real ability at it; that you may not see it in a month's play of the Amateur Championship; that the ordinary player trying to do it will most likely cut the cloth; and, finally, that only the advanced amateur should bother about it. Some authorities call it a foul, involving a kind of push. I have roughly described it, however, for the student's guidance. A final reason: you could win the Amateur Championship without even having heard of it!

SNOOKER

INTRODUCTORY

All accomplished Billiard players play a good game of Snooker, though most of them treat it as a diversion, and their attitude towards it generally is somewhat lukewarm, in some cases contemptuous. Few great Snooker players, amateur or professional, are first-class Billiard players, but the best Billiard players shine at the sister game if they take it seriously. A good Billiard player who had never touched Snooker would be able to give a good Snooker player a game, and might, given some luck, beat him over a few frames, but no Snooker player, however good, who knew nothing of Billiards, would "possess an earthly" against a real Billiard player. The inference to be drawn from this fact is—and it is a correct one—that Billiards technique includes practically every element of Snooker technique, and, moreover, the winning hazard or pot and the art of c-b control both being an integral part of Billiards, it follows logically that, as Snooker is wholly based on these, the player who has mastered Billiards technique is, by that fact, a potentially good Snooker player before he has even attempted to play the latter game.

When, therefore, as in all books which treat of both games, the lion's share of attention is given to Billiards, it does not mean that Snooker is being treated as a poor relation of the older game, but merely that the chief components of Snooker, potting and c-b control, constituting, as they do, not a part of that game, as in Billiards, but the alpha and omega, or, colloquially, the whole bag of tricks of it, and all the strokes employed in Snooker being also Billiard strokes, it follows that much less space is needed for expounding Snooker technique than for Billiards. In a word, as the whole, Billiards, contains the part, Snooker, the former must necessarily demand more attention. The art of Snooker consists of potting a ball and leaving the c-b in correct position to pot another ball. In Snooker, potting is done by plain-ball strokes, strokes with Side and Stun, Screw strokes and Follow-through strokes. Billiards contains all of these features, so it is obvious that the Billiard player has, in a technical sense, nothing new to learn when it comes to Snooker. He has but to adapt himself; the Snooker player, however, new to Billiards, has a great deal to learn, besides two new elements, losing hazards and cannon play. It is significant, in respect of the value of Billiards knowledge for the Snooker player, that Joe Davis, one of the premier giants of Billiards history, has turned out to be Snooker's greatest exponent, and that in the 1955 Amateur Snooker Championship two of the semi-finalists were Billiard players of world class, while the other two were able exponents of the game.

Joe Davis, and not only he, but also almost all great Snooker players who also play Billiards, advise the student of the sister game to learn the art of Billiards. It behoves the Snooker enthusiast, therefore, to decide for himself whether it is worth his while to do this or not. I assure him, however, that a good knowledge of Billiards technique, added to that of Snooker, i.e. in the specialized adaptation of it to the latter game, must result in his acquiring greater skill at the 22-ball game. Whether he takes kindly to the idea or not, I trust that the part of this book devoted to Billiards may be of material assistance to him, and, I should add, also to aspiring lady players, for many girls and women have taken to Snooker of recent years.

Although Billiards is played today all over Gt. Britain and throughout the Commonwealth countries, Snooker enjoys more popularity, as it is (for the ordinary player) much easier, it offers quicker results—a frame takes on an average but fifteen or twenty minutes—it enables the weaker player to have a far larger share of the game than does Billiards, and a merely competent amateur may win one or two frames even against Joe Davis; also, there being 21 object-balls on the table, and all that is necessary to do being to pot them, the players generally have something "on" (scoreable). Snooker is also extensively played in four-handed fashion (i.e. two against two), and this form of the game, allowing as it does of chit-chat, chaffing, leg-pulling, not to mention frequent refreshment—indeed four-handed snooker is frequently more of a jollification than a game—is tremendously popular.

Before the 30's, Snooker was, in professional circles, merely a device for filling up time when a player had reached his points (666) in a Billiards session, and nobody treated it as anything else. The game developed from the games of Pyramids and Pool, and Snooker was originally known as "Snooker Pool". To Joe Davis is due the elevation of Snooker into an art, as, somewhere about the early 30's, scenting its possibilities, he began to study it seriously. Prior to his doing so, the game was treated more as a potting picnic, so to speak, than anything else, but Davis realized that, by concentrating on *c-b control*, with the positional advantages that control would bring with it, Snooker could be made into a skilled game which would rival Billiards in the competitive sense, and also provide genuine entertainment to the public.

One of the chief elements in Snooker is that conveyed by its name, viz. snookering, which means the blocking of the course to the ball "on" (i.e. the ball the player is obliged to play at by the Rules) by another ball not "on" (namely, one which the Rules forbid him to play at). Davis's studies and experiments resulted in a much more subtle type of potting and snookering than that previously achieved, and as he himself began to play Snooker of a much more skilful and advanced kind than had been seen up to that time, and also to make, what had been almost unique, 100-breaks, so the game's popularity increased by leaps and bounds, with the result that today it is played by millions. The standard of play has advanced generally and, in the amateur sphere, out of all recognition.

I said that serious Billiard players, in general, infinitely prefer Billiards; even so, most of them enjoy an occasional game of Snooker as a change. And so, a game which was in past days regarded as a mere adjunct or make-weight to Billiards, has acquired independent status, and, also, as games go, genuine prestige.

HOW SNOOKER IS PLAYED

Snooker requires 22 balls, and it is, of course, played on the same kind of table as Billiards. The balls consist of the c-b (plain), used in turn by each player; 15 red balls and the colours (sometimes called "Pool balls"). These are: Black, Pink, Blue, Brown, Green and Yellow. The values are: red, 1 point; Black, 7; Pink, 6; Blue, 5; Brown, 4; Green, 3; and Yellow, 2.

The plan of the game is simple, the object being to pot all the 21 balls, and in the following manner. The player, beginning his turn or visit, aims at potting a red ball; if he succeeds, he must next try to pot one of the colours, any he chooses, and his choice will be determined by its position, that is, whether it is well placed for a pot. Should he pot a colour, he must then take a red again. Each time he pots a red ball it stays in the pocket. The coloured ball, however, is re-spotted (each colour having its own spot). This process continues until the players have disposed of the 15 reds, which means only the 6 colours remain. Having reached this stage, the colours must be potted in the following sequence: Yellow, Green, Brown, Blue, Pink and Black, and this time each colour stays down, i.e. off the table (in other words, it is *not* re-spotted).

The player who has scored more points, after the Black has been finally potted, wins the frame.

A frame consists of this potting of all the balls. A given number of frames constitutes a match.

When the game begins, the table presents the appearance depicted in D.4 (see p. 152). Before play starts, the players "string", as in Billiards, for the privilege of playing first, or of requesting the opponent to do so, but as the first stroke is an appreciable advantage (as will be seen), whoever wins the "string" always elects to play first. For his opening stroke the player may place the c-b anywhere in the "D", and he must first play at a red ball, that is, at the triangular "pack" of reds. There is no Baulk in Snooker; therefore there is no "protection" in the area enclosed by the Baulk-line, as in Billiards. The "D" area is merely the place from which a player operates at the start of the game, and also after his opponent has gone in-off, i.e. made a stroke in which his ball, the c-b, has entered a pocket, which is a foul stroke at Snooker. The Baulk-line, other than that part which forms part of the "D", is only present in Snooker because it is used in Billiards. If it were easily rubbed out, it would not, for Snooker, be there at all.

In placing the reds in pyramid fashion, a triangular frame is used. The Pink is placed on its spot, and the triangle, containing the red balls, placed (straight) with its tip as near as possible to the Pink ball without touching it.

When a player does not pot a ball, his opponent plays from the place in which the c-b has come to rest. It is legitimate if a player pots more than one red in the same stroke, but this is almost always a fluke or accident. Nevertheless, he scores 1 point for each red. Rare cases have occurred of three or four reds (or more) being so potted as the result of a "pack-smashing" stroke. It is against the Rules to pot a red and a colour or two colours (with one exception which will be mentioned later) in the same stroke. When a player makes a break in the course of which he pots all the balls on the table, he is said to have "cleared the table".

THE PENALTIES FOR INFRINGEMENTS OF THE RULES

We now come to the forfeit of points the player incurs when he breaks the Rules. The minimum penalty is 4 points; consequently, any breach of the Rules in which a red or the Yellow, Green and Brown are concerned will incur a penalty, not of 1, 2, 3 and 4 respectively, but of 4 in all cases. With Blue, Pink and Black, however, if involved in a foul, the player is mulcted to the extent of 5, 6 and 7 respectively.

Bearing this fact in mind, we are able to calculate the chief penalties the player is liable to forfeit:

(1) For missing the ball "on" (i.e. the ball the Rules require him to play "on") and hitting no other ball;

(2) For missing the ball "on" and striking a ball *not* "on";

(3) For the player's ball (the c-b) entering a pocket;

(4) For forcing a ball off the table;

(5) For pocketing by the same stroke, or for striking simultaneously, two balls other than two reds or the ball "on" and the "Nominated" ball (this is the exception mentioned on p. 141);

(6) For pocketing any ball not "on".

The penalty is assessed as follows: Forfeit of a minimum of 4 points; *or* the value of the ball the player was "on"; *or* the value of the ball wrongfully struck; *or* the value of the ball forced off the table, wrongfully pocketed, or otherwise fouled.

Of these various alternative forfeits, the highest numerical one must be exacted, that is, if two fouls occur in the same stroke (e.g. making a losing hazard and pocketing a ball not "on") the penalty will be that which applies to the foul subject to the higher forfeit.

A few examples will show how these penalties are applied:

(1) Player, on a red, misses it, no other ball being struck: penalty, 4.

(1) Player, on Black, misses it and no other ball is struck: penalty, 7.

(2) Player, on Blue, misses it and strikes Green: penalty, 5, because value of the ball "on" is 5 (Blue), and value of the ball struck (Green), though 3, is, for penalty purposes, 4 (the minimum), as explained previously.

(2) Player, on Blue, misses it and strikes Pink: penalty, 6; value of ball "on" (Blue) is 5; of ball struck is 6 (Pink).

(2) Player, on Black, misses it and strikes a red: penalty, 7, because the value of the ball not "on" is, for forfeit purposes, 4 (the minimum), and that of the ball "on" is 7, which is the "higher numerical forfeit" of the two.

(2) Player, on Brown, strikes it, and then the c-b, in turn,

hits Black, Yellow and Blue. No foul, as Brown, the ball "on", was contacted first and it does not matter what balls are struck after the ball "on".

(2) Player, on a red, misses it and strikes Black: penalty, 7; 7, value of ball "not on", being higher than 4, penalty value of ball "on".

(3) Player, on red, strikes it but goes in-off (as in Billiards): penalty, 4.

(3) Player, on Blue, misses, and c-b enters pocket without contacting another ball: penalty, 5.

(4) Player, on red, strikes it, but the c-b is forced off the table: penalty, 4, as 4 is penalty for the red; true, the c-b and not the red is forced off, but the c-b was involved with red only.

(4) Player, on a red, strikes it, but the red strikes Black, which is forced off the table; here the choice, as always, is between the various alternatives, thus, value of ball "on" (red) is 4; of ball forced off, 7 (Black): penalty, therefore, is 7.

(5) Player, on Blue, pockets Blue and a red: penalty, 5, because the value of the ball "on" is 5 (Blue), and penalty value of the ball wrongfully pocketed (red) 4.

(5) Player, on Green, strikes Green and Black simultaneously: penalty, 7, because value of the ball "on" (Green) is 4 (forfeit value), and of the ball "wrongfully struck" (Black) 7.

N.B.—The exception mentioned in No. 5 (p. 142) will be referred to later on.

(6) As stated, in any foul, generally speaking, the highest numerical forfeit is applied.

Penalty for playing with a ball other than the c-b: 7; playing on two reds successively: 7 (as the player was on a colour after the first red, and might have selected Black).

It should be mentioned that in single fouls the first impact of the c-b governs all strokes. Example: Player, on red, strikes it and then Blue: no foul. Player, on red, misses it and strikes Blue, then Pink: foul; penalty, 5.

SNOOKERING, OR LAYING A SNOOKER

A player is said to be snookered with regard to any ball
when a direct stroke in a straight line of the c-b to any point
of such ball (this naturally means the half facing the player) is
obstructed by a ball which is not "on". A ball is "on" when the
Rules allow one to play at it; it is not "on" when the Rules do
not allow one to play at it. Thus, when we have potted a red,
any coloured ball is then "on", but not another red, and *vice
versa*. When only the colours remain, Yellow, of course, is the
ball "on", then, in succession, Green, Brown, Blue, Pink and
Black. Let us examine the value of a snooker. "To snooker"
means to bar direct access to the ball "on" by our opponent
by a stroke which leaves him with a ball, or balls, not "on" in
the path of the c-b to the ball "on". This compels him to play
at it indirectly, that is, off a cushion or cushions, and the
attempt invariably fails, as such a stroke is difficult. If he
misses the ball "on" and strikes a ball not "on", he forfeits
points, and also if he strikes no ball at all, a miss (see p. 142).
Now to illustrate a snooker. Let us suppose "A" has scored 56
points, "B" 26. "B" has potted the last red, and is, therefore,
entitled to a colour, any he pleases. If he chooses Yellow, and
pots it, *it is re-spotted*, thus it may be potted *twice in succession*.
Should he pot it in the position shown (D.1), an easy pot, he
scores 2, and if he can get position for potting it again, from
its spot, he could take the six colours as they are in good
position for potting; this would bring him 27 points. Two points
(Yellow), plus 27 (colours), plus his score, 26, would make his
total 55, so he *could not win*, as "A" is 56. He therefore
requires a "snooker", which, if "A" fails to get out of it, will
cause him to forfeit points to "B". So "B" sends the c-b to *X*,
behind Black, and Yellow to *Y*. This means that "A" cannot
make a direct stroke on Yellow, Black obstructing. Pink and
Blue also obstruct, but Black, technically (i.e. the nearest,
snookering ball to the c-b), is the ball which counts as the

snookering one. "A" must now try to contact the ball "on" (Yellow) off two cushions, as shown; he fails to hit it, and the c-b finishes at Z. The miss forfeits 4 points (see p. 142), so that "B", with 26 points, plus 4 (the forfeit), plus the colours (27), can now reach 57, and so win. "A", of course, may pot a ball or two more, thus causing "B" to have to snooker again, but the point is that "B" *can now win without a snooker*. The 4 points for the forfeit makes him 30, so he will still be 26 behind, and "A" anyway may win with such a lead. Of course, should another chance of snookering occur for "B", he will naturally take it and so draw nearer, and it must be borne in mind that snookering more often than not brings the initiative, as here, for "B", from position Z, can pot Yellow by a Stun stroke, and he will then be well placed for

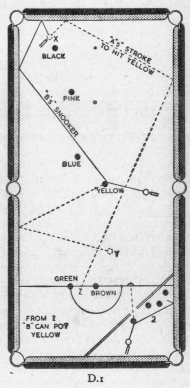

D.1

taking the other colours. On occasion, Yellow may be potted three times in succession; (1) as free-ball for the last red, (2) as Colour after red, (3) as first of the Colours.

Now snookering is not, of course, limited to such a situation as this; you may snooker at any period of the game. In fact, whenever there is no ball in pottable position, it is the game to snooker, always provided the chance of a good one exists, that is, one which will seriously handicap our opponent, for to snooker for snookering's sake, that is, to lay a snooker which can be easily got out of, is waste of time. Even if one or two balls are "on", but a risk, unjustifiable in the state of the game, is involved, it is the game to snooker. In D.1, position 2 (separated by the double line), for instance, assuming no good chance of a pot exists, a great advantage can obviously be gained by sending the red ball up the table (as the arrow indicates), and sheltering with the c-b behind the three colours shown, by a gentle stroke with running Side, thus placing our adversary in a real predicament, for we shall have made this red, and any others (which we will assume lie at the top end of the table), inaccessible by a direct stroke, so that our opponent, having to play off the bottom cushion, and perhaps the side cushions as well, is very likely to strike a ball "not on" or miss entirely, thus forfeiting points, and almost certainly leaving us a good opening.

The great value of a snooker will, therefore, be obvious from these two examples. Sometimes, near the end of a frame, more than one snooker may be required for a player to win, and, in that case, you have to decide whether to try for a snooker or to pot any balls which are "on". If you can snooker effectively, then, of course, you will do so, but, at the same time, you have to be careful not to try to snooker when it is not a certainty, as your opponent may pot enough of the balls which remain to place you decisively behind. If you cannot snooker effectively, then you must, in such a situation, keep the c-b as far away from the ball or balls "on" (for your opponent) till you can snooker with certainty. Right from the start of a frame, it is good policy to snooker whenever the chance of giving your opponent a real set-back occurs, for not only do you gain thereby the amount of his forfeit for the foul, should he, as is most probable with a genuine snooker, fail to contact the ball "on", but you will also doubtless be presented with a good opening, since he must perforce send his ball near the ball, or balls, "on", and you thus gain the initiative. A good snooker, assuming it succeeds, as it invariably does, presents you with a good leave. It is, however, bad tactics to set out to snooker as an end in itself. The means of winning is by potting balls, and the ultra-cautious player who

waits only for "certainties" merely plays into the hands of an enterprising and confident opponent. It must be remembered, however, that the game is termed Snooker, and, consequently, snookering necessarily constitutes a vital part of it. It is equivalent to tying up your opponent in order to gain openings for attack. It should certainly not be overdone but, on the other hand, it should not be overlooked, and the charge of pusillanimity that is sometimes laid against it can be brushed aside with contempt. The snooker is a deadly weapon in the hands of a skilled and calculating player and, far from

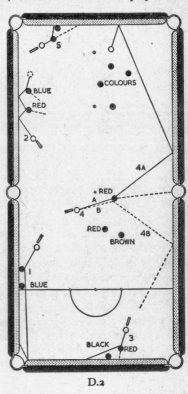

D.2

being merely defensive, is in reality a means of attack. But more of this later.

On D.2 I give five other snookers to illustrate the principle. (1) A stroke not practicable, but good practice for thin contact and testing kiss effects, also for the No. 3 type. Try it on the top cushion, not the side; (2) a cushion-first stroke, with r-h side, played very gently, places the c-b behind Blue, which snookers it on the red; a shot not to be attempted unless the need for a snooker is desperate, as the snooker is by no means certain; (3) again a skimming glance off red

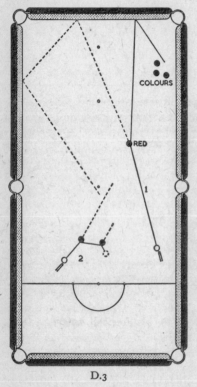

D.3

to the other side of Black; (4) potting red by a thick run-through stroke, with strong running (l-h) Side, sending the c-b behind the four colours, and, then, a snooker behind the top one. If the red we are potting here were the *last* red, and the red beside the Brown thus non-existent, it might be policy to send the red behind the colours, and the c-b behind the Brown, maybe near the bottom cushion. This would need strong r-h side (the broken line (4B) shows the stroke) as then our opponent would have to play at the red with the four colours near it, and he would be fortunate if he did not hit one of them, maybe Black or Pink, thus forfeiting 7 or 6 points; (5) sending the red to the other side of Black, and the c-b to the near side of it.

D.3: (1) A very difficult but brilliant run-through snooker, driving, by fullish contact, the red round the corner to return, as shown, and with strong running (r-h) Side, leaving the c-b behind the two colours; (2) a gentle cannon on to a colour, sending the last red ahead, and placing the c-b behind the colour, strong running (r-h) Side; this stroke presupposes the need for a snooker; otherwise we could pot red. True, the snookered ball might offer a skim contact or a cushion one, but in such a stroke the red could not be controlled and a leave (for us) would doubtless result.

THE "FREE" OR "NOMINATED" BALL

Bound up with snookering is the "Free Ball", a term you will not find in the Rules, as in them it is called the "Nominated Ball". If you snooker your opponent fairly, you, as stated previously, have gained a distinct advantage, but if you do so while making a foul stroke, such as "going in-off", striking a ball not "on", making a miss (thus contacting no ball at all) and so on, you are exposing yourself to a nasty counter-blow, as your opponent, should he, through your foul stroke, be snookered (i.e. be prevented from hitting the ball on by a direct stroke to any part of the half facing him, including the outside edges), may claim a Free ball. That is, he may nominate any colour he chooses, to serve as a red. If, for example, you snooker him on the reds by a foul stroke, he may choose, say, Brown as a red, and if he pots it he scores 1 (the value of a red), and Brown is re-spotted. He is then, of course, "on" a colour, as Brown, his Free ball, ranked as a red. If, after all the reds have been potted, you snooker your opponent, by a foul stroke, shall we say, on Green (Yellow having been potted and, of course, not brought up) he may choose any other colour as his Nominated or Free ball. If, for instance, he chooses Pink and pots it, he scores 3, the value of the ball "on" (Green, which he was snookered on by the foul), and Pink is re-spotted. When granted a Free ball, *after a foul*, the player is obliged to nominate (i.e. declare out loud, for the referee's benefit) which ball he has chosen as his Free ball, this because, if he did not do so, and his chosen ball lay near another colour, the referee would not know, if he missed his Free ball and hit the other colour, which he had really intended to select.

Although a player *must* nominate which colour he has chosen as Free ball *after a foul stroke by his opponent*, it is not obligatory for him to nominate if no foul is involved, i.e. in the ordinary course of play, and if it is obvious which colour he is intending to play, but he should do so when that colour is very near another colour, thus making it difficult for the referee to know which of the two he is "on". This is called "nominating for his own protection". Should he not do so, he incurs the risk of the referee's fouling him should he, the referee, decide the player might have played on the ball other than the one he actually struck. The referee, however, is advised by the Rules to use his discretion in the matter of nominating, whether a foul and Free ball be involved or not, that is, if the player's choice is perfectly obvious.

The reader may recall that in point No. 5 (see p. 142), I stated that the case of "striking the ball 'on' and the Nominated ball simultaneously" would be referred to later. I do so now as the ball "on" and the "Free ball" are subject to a special rule (Rule 11). Should the player, having nominated his Free ball, after a foul, strike it (the Rules require that he *must* hit the Nominated ball, in such a case), but fail to pot it, and yet pot the ball "on", he scores the value of the latter, and continues his break. Should he, however, pot both the Nominated ball and the ball "on" in the same stroke, only the ball "on" shall be "scored", and he continues; only the Nominated ball must be re-spotted. As, therefore, the Rules permit potting the Nominated ball and the ball "on" in the same stroke, it follows that they may be struck simultaneously (Rule 9) (p. 142, No. 5). If only the Nominated (or "Free") ball be potted, it scores the value of the ball "on", and is spotted.

Here are a few more points to bear in mind so far as the Rules are concerned:

If you are, after a foul stroke by your opponent, angled (by the pocket jaw), you may play "from hand", i.e. from the

"D", and if *then* you are snookered, you may claim a Free ball, but you may not do so from the angled position.

You must not make an "intentional" miss if snookered.

If the c-b is touching a ball which is "on", you must play away from it, but must not move it. You may make a miss, or may strike another ball, and you may also pot any ball which is "on", except, of course, the actual and touching ball "on", as in the latter instance you would be making a "push", which is a foul.

If the c-b is touching a ball which is *not* "on", you must likewise play away from it, but you must hit the ball "on", and no other ball; otherwise you incur a penalty.

You must *not* snooker with the ball you nominate after being fouled, that is, with a Free ball.*

You *must* hit the Nominated ball, after receiving a Free ball.

When only the Black is left, the game is ended if (a) a player pots it or (b) makes a foul stroke (e.g. goes in-off it, etc.). If, furthermore, a player, having potted it, draws level with the 7 points he secures, the Black is re-spotted and the players draw lots for choice of stroke. Afterwards, the first score or forfeit (i.e. foul stroke) ends the game, as (a) and (b).

With this preliminary survey of the scheme of Snooker dealt with, and having taken a look at some of the more important rules, we may proceed to the game itself.

THE OPENING STROKE

As in Billiards, players open the game in one of two ways. The one adopted by first-class amateurs and professionals is that shown in D.4 From the "D" we play straight at the outside red of the four-ball of reds, contacting it a good h-b, with strong running Side; the c-d takes the course shown, passing the Blue with something to spare, and finishing (as shown) either on the bottom cushion or rebounding a little according to the strength used. The stroke releases two or

---

* You must not snooker with the nominated or free ball after being fouled, unless only Black and Pink are left on the table. Also you may snooker on a red, other reds being snookered by other colours.

three red balls, and if the c-b has remained on or close to the bottom cushion, or rebounded off it to a position behind Green, Brown or Yellow, our opponent will have a very awkward situation left, possibly being snookered on any of the reds, and then having to play (indirectly) up the table, i.e. off a cushion or cushions. If so, he is likely to leave the c-b advantageously placed for us, and as our first stroke released some reds, we may have an opening from his stroke. If no opening is presented, we shall still be ideally placed for making another defensive or "safety" stroke, off a red, back to the bottom cushion area, probably giving the opponent yet another stiff problem. The reader will see by these remarks how very important is this opening stroke, and indeed it can lead, and very often has led, to a winning leave. A perfectly played opening stroke is, therefore, tantamount to gaining the initiative at the very outset as the opponent may have to face either an awkward snooker, if the c-b ends up behind a "D" colour, or an uncomfortable stroke with the c-b tucked up against the bottom cushion, and possibly both of these difficulties!

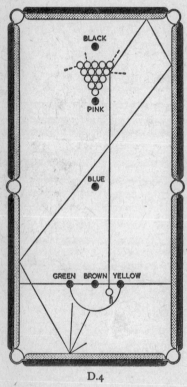

D.4

Opening stroke 2 is shown in D.5. This consists of striking the end red of the top row of reds, not h-b, but a bit finer, and without any Side. The c-b returns as depicted, passing outside the Yellow. A h-b contact or thicker than fine ball may result in the c-b's colliding with Brown, or a too thin one, with Yellow, which, of course, is a bad stroke in either case. Playing the other stroke (D.4), there is a possibility of disturbing Blue if the necessary sharp turning of the top r-h corner is not achieved by the requisite degree of running Side, or if a too fine contact (i.e. less than h-b) is made. No. 1 opening releases more reds than No. 2, as the stroke requires more force, and the reds released in both cases will probably be on the opposite side of the Pyramid or Pack to that contacted by the c-b. Nearly all players play, instinctively, both

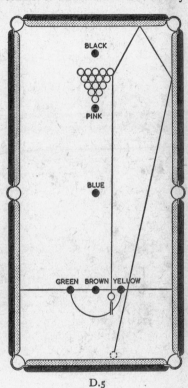

D.5

these openings on the r-h side of the table. No. 1 opening (D.4) sometimes results in the c-b's travelling near or into the bottom l-h pocket if, instead of the correct ball (the end one of the four-ball row), the end red of the third row is struck, but here again such a danger does not exist if the stroke be properly played. Some players still use No. 2 opening (D.5), but the preference is strongly in favour of No. 1 (D.4). In using running Side for opening stroke 1, do not forget that the aim should not be on the thin side, as the Side will make the contact less thick than that we aim for (see "Side", p. 46).

The opening stroke in Snooker, therefore, is no mere formality, like kicking-off in football; rather does it resemble the first ball in cricket, which may take a wicket. Many a frame at Snooker has been lost through a bad opening stroke, which resulted in sending a red or two over a top-pkt, or which, being too forceful, came off the bottom cushion, to stop *above* the "D" colours. The stroke which dislodges some red balls may leave your opponent with a good opening, and having potted a red, he may in potting the next ball, a colour, be able to upset the Pyramid of reds, and thereby create an ideal opening for a good break, or he may be able to rob us of the initiative which the opening stroke provides. The opening stroke can mean our getting in the first blow. Hence its great importance.

POTTING AT SNOOKER

As potting in both Billiards and Snooker means the same thing, that is, pocketing the o-b with the c-b to leave the latter in position for another scoring stroke, it is obvious that, having dealt with the theory of potting in the Billiards section of this book, there can be little to add to what has been said on the subject, at least, so far as potting itself is concerned. It does so happen that we find Billiard players who pot well at Billiards yet not so well at Snooker, and also Snooker players whose potting at Billiards, if they play it as a diversion, is far from the standard of their Snooker potting. This is probably due, in each case, to the player's being much more at home in the game he specializes in. In other words he knows to a far greater extent what he is aiming at positionally when potting. Potting at Snooker does consist of more Stun and Screw strokes than at Billiards, though in the Top-of-the-table game both these are constantly needed; in all-round or open Billiards we do not have to employ this style of pot so often. Snooker in general demands a different touch, owing to this predominant element of Stun, and, if possible, a different cue, though few players who play both games use different cues. Most Billiard players use a $17\frac{1}{2}$-oz. cue. Joe Davis recommends a $16\frac{1}{2}$-oz. cue for Snooker, but different players favour different weights, Clark McConachy, for instance, favouring a 21-oz. cue! Personally, I favour a shorter cue for either game than that generally used—most cues are 4 ft. 10 in. in length—and a 16- or $16\frac{1}{2}$-oz. cue for Snooker. It is important that the player find the ideal cue for his physique and style and, therefore, it is really impossible to fix on weight, dimensions, etc., for others. I mention this matter here as a cue lasts a lifetime, and to play with the cue which best suits one's special requirements is all-important. As scoring at Snooker is all potting, the Snooker player should experiment with the large number of cues at his disposal in the hall or club where he plays until he picks up one which to him seems to fit in perfectly for potting with his style and physique. He should then, after thoroughly satisfying himself that that is indeed his cue, buy it or have one made exactly like it.

To revert to potting at Snooker, if there is any difference between potting at Billiards and Snooker, it lies in the fact that the Snooker player has to make most of his pots by Stun and Screw effects and, therefore, he has the problem more frequently of having to aim at positional precision in making such pots. In other words, his potting strokes are subject to this complication to a much greater extent in Snooker than in Billiards, and often at longer distances, for, though the Top-of-the-table player has also to get perfect position when making the Stun and Screw pots that phase of Billiards calls for, he executes such strokes within a more restricted area, round the Spot. In Snooker, however, the second ball to be potted may lie a long way off the first. Nevertheless, the fact remains that if you can pot well at one game, you should be able, with due adaptation, to pot well at the other, assuming you play it regularly. Consequently, if you have assimilated the theory of potting given on pp. 31, 32, and practised hard, there is nothing radically new to learn about potting at Snooker. As, however, Snooker is nothing but potting, all Billiard players can profit by playing seriously at it, just as Snooker players can learn a great deal about Side, angles and ball control in general, by taking Billiards seriously. Naturally, if any serious competitive games are to be played at one game or the other, the particular game which is to be played competitively should be played exclusively at the time; that is, the two should not then be intermixed, and most players concentrate on one or the other.

The prime idea the Snooker player must get into his head right from the start is: potting must always be positional; in other words, a pot must never be made without leaving the c-b accurately for potting the next ball, which means c-b control is what distinguishes the first-class Snooker player. I therefore recommend the serious aspirant to Snooker honours, during his graduation stage, which must be necessarily a very long one, to play, as practice, always a number of frames with positional considerations primarily in mind, and if he can find a colleague to co-operate with him in this, they will both not delay long in advancing along the path of positional Snooker skill. In such games, they should not worry about missing the pot provided they have secured position.

It is a good plan, when going to pot a ball, to begin by getting down low in order to "take your angle", that is, determine the point to contact on the o-b to make the pot. Having fixed this —I am referring to fairly close range pots, not to long pots— *you may forget about the pocket* and concentrate on striking the point on the o-b on the spot you have fixed upon. The eye, however, should not alternate between pocket, o-b and c-b, but should be riveted on the aforesaid contact point (o-b), with, if found necessary, a last-moment confirming glance. Your eye should be fixed, as I say, on the o-b, as you make your stroke, and, of course, on the point on it to be contacted (see Billiards Section, Ds.3, 11). The difficulty of potting, however, lies in the fact that, although your eye is fixed on this point, you must not aim at it (i.e. with the cue), for the points of contact and aim are not the same! They differ by half a ball's width. D.6 (1) (as also D.7), makes this clear. The line from the pocket centre, *P—C*, must run through the centre, *C*, of the o-b, for the pot to be made; therefore, the c-b, at the moment of contact, must have been directed in such a way that *its* centre,

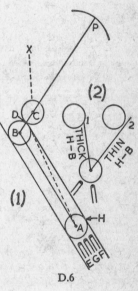

B, meets the line from the pocket at half a ball's width from the point at which the two balls make contact, namely *D*, and this centre of the c-b, *B*, must, as shown, lie on the straight line from the pocket, *P—C*. We cannot, therefore, achieve this end by aiming through *A*, the c-b's centre, at the point of contact on the o-b, *D* (see broken line), for, if we did, we should send the o-b in *X* direction. To put it another way, we have to make the outside edge of the c-b, *H*, travel along the line *H—D*, thus making the same contact, as if we aim through *A*, c-b's centre, at *B*. The cue aim, *G*, is, as is ob-

D.6

vious, the plain-ball pot; *E* represents the pot, with l-h side, *F*, with r-h side, and when imparting Side, in potting, we must, as is clear, keep our cue aim parallel, not diagonal, with line *A—B*, which is that of the plain-ball pot. In short, all pots must be made from the centre of the c-b to the *point of aim*, not to the point of contact, except, of course, in a dead straight pot. In the case of pots for which we have a definite aiming-point, i.e. ¼-b, h-b and ¾-b pots, the task is simplified. The reader should read the section on potting in the Billiards part of this book (pp. 30–38) as these angles and throw-offs are illustrated there, and that section amplifies the present one. If I were asked the secret of potting, I should advise: first, study the theory, then master the three angles just referred to, and, thirdly, practise pots from all angles, at short and long distances, being sure, however, not to make them successively, but so many times separately.

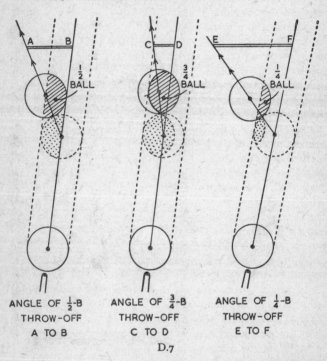

ANGLE OF ½-B
THROW-OFF
A TO B

ANGLE OF ¾-B
THROW-OFF
C TO D

ANGLE OF ¼-B
THROW-OFF
E TO F

D.7

When, by practice, we have the quarter, half and three-quarter contacts and lines or angles of the o-b's course, in each case, in our mind's eye, we can vary each slightly to make pots which are slightly "off" such angles or contacts. Thus we may require a thick or a thin h-b contact. In the diagram (D.6 (2)) I show the aim for a thick and a thin h-b pot.

No. 1 (thick) shows the aim must be slightly within the edge (which latter, of course, is the h-b aim); No. 2 (thin) shows it must be slightly outside it. If, as it should be, the h-b pot angle is firmly in our mind, we may by these adjustments provide for pots which lie slightly off or inside the h-b stroke. Potting is, in fact, the product of continued practice and the memorizing of angles and contacts. Most amateurs pot by eye alone, by knack or intuitively, call it what you will, that is, without having made any systematic study of the art. The wise student will study the matter, and he will thus attain consistency, which is, except a player be a born potter, what the instinctive potter fails in.

In long pots, of course, it is far from easy to concentrate on the precise point of contact, as in short-range potting, but the

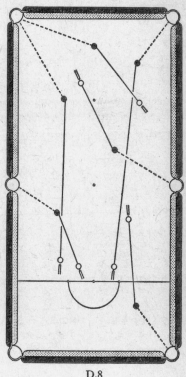

D.8

theory remains true, and, in any case, however distant a pot may be, we still enjoy the advantage of having the basic contacts and angles ($\frac{1}{4}$-b, h-b and $\frac{3}{4}$-b) firmly photographed in our mind's eye, and by mental adjustment of these angles, coupled with the straight-line pot, we may, even in long pots, benefit from theoretical knowledge and achieve accuracy.

Moreover, in long-range potting, our vision embraces both pocket and the o-b in one comprehensive grasp, as everything is foreshortened at such range. Even the greatest players often miss pots and sometimes miss quite a lot of them: it follows

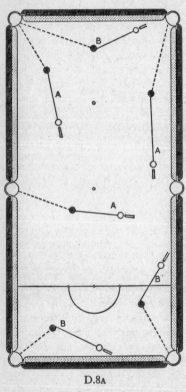

D.8A

then that no matter what the potting system the player may employ, none is infallible. If it were, Snooker would cease to be a game! True cueing, again, is the chief aid, and, of course, good eyesight is indispensable. In all long pots, as a rule Screw, Stun, etc., are advisable, except when we wish the c-b to travel some distance after contact. Straight long pots, however, should be made by Stun; angular long pots at fair pace, and with decision. In potting a ball at distance, say more than 6 ft., and especially in a hard-hitting stroke, the player often, at the crucial moment, alters his line

of aim in a sort of wild smash at the ball; control of aim should be borne in mind in all such strokes. The good long-range potter maintains cue-control in such strokes, and this is indispensable. Practice is, of course, quite invaluable and, in fact, is the ultimate secret of good potting. Long potting, therefore, must be assiduously practised, and all theories of potting are useless unless practice is constant. True cueing and regular practice, allied to care of the sight, and health, will do as much as anything to develop the potting gift, but the theory, of course, must be understood.

D.7 depicts $\frac{1}{4}$-b, h-b and $\frac{3}{4}$-b contacts, angles and the throw-off of the potted ball in each case. Thus the double-line A—B is the angle of the throw-off of the o-b in h-b contact; C—D, that in the $\frac{3}{4}$-b contact, and E—F, that in the $\frac{1}{4}$-b contact. These angles should be committed to memory and constantly practised. Aim in the h-b contact is, of course, at the edge of the o-b; in the $\frac{3}{4}$-b contact, at a point half-way between the centre and edge of the o-b, and, in the $\frac{1}{4}$-b contact, at a point a $\frac{1}{4}$-b outside the o-b. D.8: Some h-b pots; D.8A: A, some $\frac{3}{4}$-b pots; B, some $\frac{1}{4}$-b pots.

STUN, STAB AND SCREW

In the early days of Snooker, the plain-ball pot (i.e. a centrally struck c-b, i.e. without Side, etc., with the cue following on) was the rule. Nowadays, owing to the development of c-b control, or positional play in Snooker, Stun and Screw have acquired supreme importance in potting, since by means of them the c-b can be handled, positionally speaking, with so much greater precision. In a game involving so many balls in so many positional relationships, close and distant, it would not be possible to execute without Stun, Screw and Stab Strokes the sharp diagonal angles and the awkward circular movements which are necessary, either to direct the c-b in accordance with such requirements, or to cause it to remain nearby. By Stun and Screw the c-b can be controlled within a small radius or sent a distance. Without the aid of Stun and Screw the c-b would stray far beyond, or fall short of, the intended spot, and direction would be greatly restricted.

With reds round the Black or Pink balls, on, or near, their spots, Stun and Screw enable the c-b to be kept nearby, displace the o-b, or remain in the same place, and thus all angles are "negotiable". These two balls are the most lucrative for break-making, and Black-red and Pink-red sequences form the basis of big breaks. Playing on the Pink, four pockets (the two top and the two centre) are at one's disposal. In Black-and-red play, which is a derivative of the Top-of-the-table game at Billiards, Stun and Screw enable the player to get position on one ball or the other on the same, or the opposite, side of the table. Both these strokes have been dealt with in the Billiards section and do not need further extensive treatment. Briefly recapitulating, the Stun Stroke requires low striking of the c-b, though not so low as in Screw, fullish contact on the o-b, a sharp, crisp delivery, no follow-through and a firm cue-hold. It is easier than the Screw Stroke. Stab is much the same in essence, and if you can execute the Stun Stroke you can execute Stab. For all practical purposes there is scarcely any difference between the two. Technically, the Stun Stroke leaves the c-b in the near vicinity of the o-b; the Stab Stroke causes it to displace the o-b, remaining on the spot the latter occupied. To do this, of course, contact must be dead full; for Stun, it need not be.

Nearly all players, when learning to screw back, fail to follow-through with the cue and the c-b, instead of recoiling, stays more or less where it was. Thus what has been done is none other than the Stun Stroke, although not intended. Whenever you wish the c-b to displace the o-b, stop dead nearby or trickle into a nearby position, you employ Stab or Stun. A minimum of recoil cancels out forward momentum. A shortened cue-hold aids in Stun Strokes when the o-b is close. Generically, Stun and Screw are little removed from each other. The function of both is to take momentum out of the c-b. For all practical purposes we may treat Stun and Stab as one, for what else is the Stab Stroke to displace the o-b by the c-b but a Stun Stroke? Stab is Stun with absolutely full contact. You execute both strokes alike. A Stun Stroke, with the o-b at a distance, requires some recoil effect, and this, coupled with the dead resistance of the o-b, kills forward movement. You will find it useful to take your bridge a little nearer for a Stun shot. If you can screw back, all you have to do to stun is to check follow-through with the cue. Stun is allied to Screw, and when you stun you are partially screwing without screw-back effect, and also contacting the o-b in a weightier manner than with Screw. Everything in Screw or Stun must be firm, the bridge and the cue-hold, yet not clumsy. There must be no snatching or jabbing effect, all must be neat and controlled. In proportion as direct screw-back effect is less desired, so must cue follow-through be diminished. Moreover, good cue follow-through, with low contact, of course, pro-motes a strong recoil, which we do not want in many Stun Strokes, a mere lateral move-ment of the c-b (from say 3–9 in.) being all that is desired.

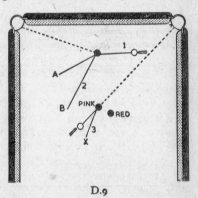

Stun can be used with less than full con-tact (see D.9, No. 1). By stunning the Black (on its spot) we par-tially run through it,

D.9

to *A*, to get the other side. This stroke, a Stun pot at Billiards, is useful for getting to *B* (No. 2) for a cross loser into the r-h top-pkt; No. 3 is a Stun pot of Pink; wishing to get well on the adjacent red, we apply some screw-back effect, and some check (l-h) Side (Pink should be struck a fraction off centre, to enter the pocket at the arrow position). From *X*, we would pot the red with Stun, remaining fairly straight for the subsequent Stun pot of Pink into the l-h pocket. The reader will perceive the value of Stun for playing a Pink-and-red sequence. In such a sequence we may sometimes use the cush-ion(s), but mostly Stun or Screw will be the medium. When a ball is on the verge of a pocket, and we wish to prevent the c-b from following on into the pocket, we employ the Stab Stroke, leaving the c-b in the o-b's previous position. Though we strike the c-b lower for screw-back puposes than for Stun, when stunning at a distance, a little screw-back effect is useful to make up for the distance the c-b has to travel, and the distance will cancel out any pronounced backward recoil of the c-b after contact. We can, there-

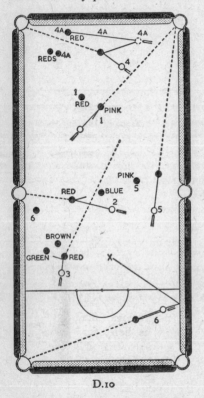

fore, in a long-range Stun Stroke, contact the c-b (with our cue) as low as we do for screwback effect. In close or fairly close Stun shots, however, you must not strike the c-b as low as for Screw, as stated, and you will be able to check your contact by what the c-b does. Get the idea of Stun, which is the transfer of force from the c-b to the o-b, into your head and you will capture the knack. Employ the forearm as your main instrument. So remember, a sharp, incisive stroke, and *no* follow-through of the cue.

D.10 shows some Stun and Screw Strokes used in Snooker. (1) Stun pot of Pink, with slight screw-back effect, to get on red, and also to steer clear of the Pink Spot when the latter ball is re-spotted. When potting a ball near one of the colour Spots, care should always be taken to visualize the afterposition of the c-b so that it will not remain on such a spot, or hamper the next stroke by overlapping it; (2) Stun pot of red

D.10

to get on Blue; (3) Stun Stroke on red to send it up the table, and to place the c-b behind Brown or Green for a Snooker; (4) Stun Stroke, potting Black and going to position 4A, for potting red near the top cushion; in this position we should if possible cause the c-b to rebound off the cushion to separate the two reds (4A), as we cannot, subsequently, make use of them for potting, each obstructing the other. We should constantly have an eye to this subsidiary function of potting, provided the stroke itself is not thereby jeopardized. In this type of stroke (4A, red pot) we may want to come *straight* off the cushion to get on the Black; if so, we must apply some check (r-h) Side; if we want the c-b to travel forward diagonally off the cushion in the direction of the side cushion we would employ running (l-h) Side; (5) Stun pot of red to displace the red for position on Pink (pot into opposite mid-pkt); (6) screw-back pot of colour, with l-h side, to assist rebound off cushion to X, for potting red (6). Refer to p. 33 for explanation of this Side effect (D.12).

The "Soft Screw" is one of the most delicate and exacting strokes in Snooker or Billiards. This stroke is invaluable in getting position on reds when potting the Black, it being possible, with the c-b fairly close to the Black, to place the latter at any angle round the former. This gentle Screw is something of a knack, and not to be mastered impromptu, as it were. It requires a delicate touch, the cue to be held lightly and the strength to be controlled, the motive force being really centred in the finger-tips and the wrist, with the latter moving freely and flexibly, but not loosely. The maximum range for the Soft Screw is about $2\frac{1}{4}$ ft. The actual action consists of a deft little forward movement of the cue, and a sudden checking of it at the instant of impact, and, of course, a low point of tip-contact. The checking must not, however, come before contact, as this will destroy the purposeful action which the stroke demands. Confidence is essential, too, for being scared of the stroke will result in a merely clumsy action. Whether you are screwing back or off the straight or sideways, the stroke is not different in kind, as a lateral Screw simply means a lateral point of contact instead of a central (on the o-b), and here I must warn against always relying on Side to obtain direction, as, in most cases, the latter, in short-distance Screws, is obtainable by varying the point of contact. When, however, a pronounced curve is required in direction, Side is essential. Also, if we must strike centrally, as is un-avoidable if the pot is a dead straight one, then, to leave the c-b to the side instead of in a straight line with the ball we are potting, Side is necessary to get off the straight line, as we saw in D.9, stroke 3. This Soft Screw Stroke is as important as any in the game for it enables the player to keep "on top of" the ball or balls "on", which, in its turn, is one of the main requisites in good Snooker. Often a cluster of pottable balls lies in a small area, and the c-b, by Soft Screws and Stuns, has to be delicately manœuvred within that area, the various pots demanding little "wriggling" movements or sharp turns of the c-b within a radius of from an inch or so to a foot and more.

BREAKING THE PACK

What is known as the "Deep Screw" Stroke is rather a different proposition. It is, of course, a Screw Stroke played with force, and it is used, among other things, for breaking the pack of reds, while potting a colour, or even a red, also for screw-back from a distant o-b. While the pack is more or less solid (i.e. intact) with only one or two or three reds, separated from it, it is of no use for scoring, and, therefore, it is necessary to break it up at the first opportunity, though, naturally, we must only attempt this in conjunction with an actual pot, which, of course, presupposes that one, two or more reds were loose; for otherwise we should not have anything to pot. To try to split the pack, in a non-potting stroke would, of course, be very risky, for our opponent may get the benefit.

We can smash the pack either when potting a red (risky as we shall see) or a colour. As we pot the particular ball, we, at

the same time, try to cannon into the pack and, in the previous
stroke, we should, while making *that* pot, have made it our
purpose to get into position for the pot which is to enable us to
disturb the pack in accordance with the latter purpose. We
can, therefore, utilize
any pot which crops up,
as it were, to send the
c-b into the pack, if
position permits, or we
can manœuvre to make
the next pot suitable.

D.11 depicts pack-
smashing strokes. We
have potted an odd red,
and got to position *A*
or *B*. From *A*, we pot
Black with a fairly forceful Screw Stroke and,
with a little l-h side,
the c-b is turned into
the clustered reds to
separate as many as
possible for potting;
from *B*, simply play a
forcing h-b stroke off
the cushion with l-h
Side, and at a fair
pace, to rebound into
the reds. The positions
A and *B* are the "stock"
ones to aim at placing

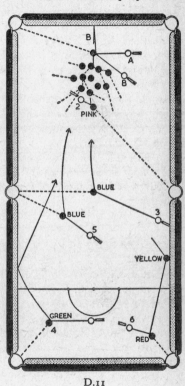

D.11

the c-b in when potting a red in a top-pkt, with the object
of smashing into the pack when potting Black. No. 3 shows
a deep Screw Stroke with a little r-h side, to pot Blue and
Screw into the reds (as shown); (5) the same stroke with a
little r-h side, with Blue away from its spot; (4) potting Green
with a strong Screw and some r-h side, to crash the c-b into

the reds off the side cushion (a difficult stroke). No. 2 shows
Pink potted by a Screw Stroke, l-h side, with the c-b turned
into the reds. No. 6 is a crisp Screw shot, with slight l-h side,
to pot the last red and bring the Yellow into the open; some
Stun enables us to slow up the c-b so as not to send Yellow
more than a foot or two. In the diagram the reds are loosely
situated, but it is just as necessary to separate them as it is
when the pack is fairly solid, as they obstruct each other so far
as potting possibilities are concerned. Blue, on its spot, offers
the danger of the c-b glancing off a red at the side of the pack
into a top-pkt, especially when the pack is more or less intact,
but, all the same, it is a good ball to use for splitting the pack,
and there are many occasions when it can be effectively used,
by a deep Screw Stroke, to break up the pack. To Screw off
the Green, Brown or Yellow, on or near their spots, to break
the pack, whether direct or off a side cushion (as in No. 4), is
very difficult and risky, as you may pot a ball not "on", or the
c-b may go in-off another ball. To try to break the pack while
potting a red is seldom the game because the c-b may land in
the midst of the reds, and as you are then "on" a colour, you
may be "snookered", as it were, on the colours. Therefore the
colours are the best balls wherewith to "do the trick", as, if
you finish amongst reds, you will, at worst, be able, almost
always, to make a defensive stroke off a red to the top or
bottom of the table. The deep or forcing Screw sometimes
needs Side, when the angle is wide, in which case the c-b will
take a curved course, as indeed it generally will, in any long
Screw Strokes (as D.29, "Billiards", shows). To sum up, Black
is the best ball off which to smash or disturb the pack reds.
Naturally, you cannot control the c-b at any distance in a
forcing Screw Stroke unless contact is fairly full, the minimum
contact being a thickish h-b, but for controlling direction at
least $\frac{3}{4}$-b contact is necessary. It goes without saying that we
break up or disturb the "pack" for our own benefit and not for
our opponent's, so we must be very careful not to select a pot
which we may miss, thus letting our opponent reap the benefit.
The pack can, of course, be split by any type of stroke, i.e. by

Screw, a forcing stroke, a plain-ball stroke off one or more cushions, and so on. The *bouclée* bridge (p. 54) is mostly used for deep screwing.

Although Stun and Screw play such a large part in Snooker, of course, many other types of stroke are employed, including the plain-ball stroke. A very useful stroke in Snooker is the Run-through, and it serves admirably for both potting and snookering. Suppose, for example, we wished, in position 5 of D.11, to pot a red, instead of Blue, into the mid-pkt, and to get on the Black, we would run-through the red, with running (r-h) Side, and the c-b would contact the side and top cushions, to run into position on the Black. And, with regard to snookering and the Run-through stroke, an example will be seen in D.12, No. 1. Here we have potted a red, and require two snookers to stand a chance of winning. The last red is in the vicinity of the top l-h pocket. With strong r-h side, we run thickly through the Blue, and the Side takes the c-b off the bottom cushion to a spot behind the three colours, a formidable snooker for our opponent. We could not pot the Blue, as the Pink obstructs. We might have got the same position by a thin stroke off Blue, but by bringing Blue back, as shown, we create a further obstacle for our opponent when he comes to try to hit the red.

THE DOUBLE

The double is a very useful stroke, and it can be made into both mid-pkts and top-pkts, although only the once-across-the-table double into a mid-pkt can be called at all sure, and even that can easily be missed! The double is "on" whether the o-b lie touching the cushion or an inch or two away from it.

D.12, stroke 2: An ordinary mid-pkt double with the o-b on the cushion. Naturally, this stroke is not "on" when c-b and o-b are almost straight; the example shown represents about the limit at which the double can be made, as, at a lesser angle than here, a kiss will result. The mistake of the average player is the idea he has that doubles must be made with a bang, as it were, that is, at great pace. When the angle is narrow, speed is necessary to escape the kiss, and in this case the double should be made at strong pace. Often the pocket aimed at is missed, and the o-b travels across off the cushion to enter the opposite pocket; most players take this for granted, reasoning that if it misses one, it will probably enter the other, but in first-class Snooker such a "double-double" is a fluke. There is, however, a position in which the double-double is a legitimate objective, and this occurs when a ball blocks the way to the pocket for the single double (see No. 5, where Blue (5) blocks the direct double). We then play to make the o-b hit the opposite cushion so that it strikes it at a point to

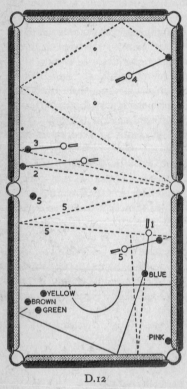

D.12

carry it into the pocket on the other side (i.e. the one on the same side as the o-b lies). The art of the double, of course, lies in correctly gauging the angle of rebound, and this will be learned with experience. The main concern in doubling is controlled pace, as opposed to the crash policy. Stroke 3 is a double, with the o-b, away from the cushion. A little harder, as the angle *on* to the cushion has to be taken into account, but the same principle of judging the rebound applies. If the once-across double approaches the straight, some Side to take the c-b out of the path of the o-b is necessary, and naturally in No. 2 stroke, if we thought a kiss might occur, we should use r-h side, causing the c-b to veer to the right. No. 4 is what is called the "cocked hat" double; though never a certainty even with the best players, it can generally be tried, as, if the pocket is missed, no harm is done as the c-b, having to be stunned, remains safe. The double is often a Stun Stroke, particularly when the o-b is on the cushion, and, of course, whether it lies on or just away from the cushion, we may want the c-b to stay nearby, and this needs a Stun or Screw Stroke. Advanced doubles are those shown in D.13. Nos. 1 and 2 are Stun doubles; practice will give knowledge of the angle throw-offs in such positions; (3) a doubling into the mid-pkt, and directing, with some check (l-h) Side, of the c-b into position on the Black; (4) a difficult cut double, but without undue risk, as we may bring the c-b back, as shown. There are countless other positions which allow doubling. Do not forget that ex-cessive pace is, generally speaking, not needed in doubles; neither is *insufficient* pace when there is a likelihood of a leave being left for the opponent if the stroke fails. If the situation is "tight", discretion must be used in doubling, but in "dis-tant" doubles (such as Nos. 1, 2 and 4, D.13) there is no great risk entailed, as we leave the c-b far away from the o-b, a prime principle of Snooker defensive play, though not neces-sarily of snookering.

SIDE IN SNOOKER

Side plays its part in Snooker despite the dominance of Stun and Screw. In Black-and-red sequences Side is needed, and that for obvious reasons, when we remember that red-and-Black play is a by-product of the Top-of-the-table game and the reader will, by this time, know how important Side

is in that phase of Billiards. The stroke, No. 3 on D.13, needed
check (l-h) Side, as stated, in order to narrow the angle of
the c-b's rebound from the cushion, to get on Black: we might
have used running (r-h) Side, but, in that case, would have

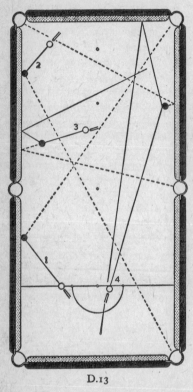

had to contact the top
and r-h side cushions,
but why make the
stroke more complica-
ted?

D.14, No. 1, shows a
snooker in which run-
ning Side plays the
dominant part. Contact-
ing the red thickly to
take the force out of the
c-b, we apply all the
Side we can and thus
get a very wide angle of
rebound off the bottom
cushion to shelter be-
hind the four colours.
(2) No red is "on", so,
the one shown at X
being the only red ball
we can safely play on to
return to the bottom
area, we contact it on
its l-h side, with all the
check (r-h) Side we can
muster, which causes
the c-b to rebound from

D.13

the top and side cushions at the angle shown, and return. Had
we not applied this Side, the c-b would have collided with the
two colours and stayed at the top to our disadvantage. There
is a chance of a "shot to nothing" (D.19) double here, as
shown by the broken line. (3) Here we do not wish to pot red,
being well behind, but to obtain a snooker. We therefore wish

to drive red off the top and side cushions behind one of the colours (referred to in stroke 2), as shown by the broken line (the arrow represents the direction not the stopping-place of the red), and, to do this, we must contact it (the red) full to

so direct it, but, in do-
ing that, we have a
wider angle to surmount
in order to snooker be-
hind the two colours, at
Y, than if we contacted
red thinly, which we
cannot do as we should
leave it near the top-
pkt. We therefore use
good strength, to im-
part speed to the red,
and apply the strongest
possible running (l-h)
Side, to come off the
top cushion at a wide
angle. The stroke is a
run-through of red, and
it illustrates both the
value of Side and the
thick run-through,
which gives pace to the
o-b and stays that of the
c-b. (4) An easy pot of
red is "on"; we see, how-
ever, that lying near to
the l-h top side cushion

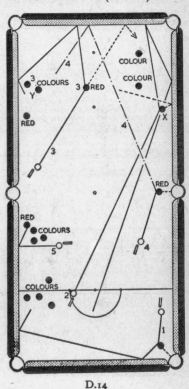

D.14

is the last red, quite "safe" (i.e. out of play), so, by using strong running (l-h) Side, we pot the red, and the c-b, off the top cushion (as shown by line (4)), travels to the last red, and, as we use good pace, will probably bring it out into the open. This stroke illustrates the use of the cannon in Snooker. Without strong Side this angle would have been impossible to achieve. Whenever we have a certain pot on, and perceive a ball or balls lying safe, we should consider whether it is feasible to "rescue" them, as in this cannon stroke. (5) By using strong r-h side we contact the snookered red, which we could not do without it.

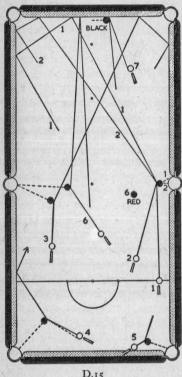

D.15

THE CUT

In this stroke the o-b is struck with the finest of contacts. If, for example, the c-b is 2 ins. away from the r-h side cushion, say on the Baulk-line (D.15, No. 1), and there is a red 2 in. from the edge of the r-h mid-pkt, it is obvious that in such a position we can pot it, if at all, only by grazing the outside edge of it with the c-b. The farther the o-b lies from the pocket in such a position, the faster will be the pace necessary to cut it in, and unless there is a clear course for the c-b, it may collide with one or more balls with unfavourable results. Another risk in the Cut Stroke is missing the o-b altogether, which will not only involve a penalty for the miss but, what is worse, leave a "sitter" for our opponent. It is, therefore, advisable to make sure of contacting the o-b, also of avoiding other balls in the vicinity. A Cut involving more than half the length of the table is not a safe risk to take unless well ahead. If the pocket is fully open the Cut Stroke is well "on", but if it is a blind, or semi-blind, pocket, caution is the rule. Cuts are not always of the glancing kind; a $\frac{1}{4}$-b contact is, in essence, a Cut. It is advisable, therefore, to practise this stroke in positions involving the thinnest of contacts up to the $\frac{1}{4}$-b contact. If it is necessary to impart running Side (stroke 2) with the nap for positional purposes, in cutting a ball, allowance must, of course, be made for the pull of the Side before it reaches the o-b but Side for the Cut should not be applied for any but short distances. The Cut is very useful for defensive purposes, in an "on-the-Black" duel, for instance, when, with Black lying on the cushion (No. 7), we wish to leave it there. By just grazing it, we can send the c-b to the other end of the table and leave the Black safe. We often find a ball near a corner pocket in "cuttable" position, but lying a foot or so out from the pocket. This Cut necessitates going round the table, and we must then be careful not to collide with other balls, and also to avoid going in-off. D.15: (1) A fine cut, sending the c-b to position on Pink (at 1), with a trifle of l-h (running) Side (allow for this in aiming) to come off the top cushion as shown; this pot represents the maximum angle at which a cut is possible—i.e. a trifle less than a right angle— here, the angle is a little *greater* than a right angle, but we can offset that as the o-b is so near the pocket that we can pot it off the shoulder, as shown; (2) cutting red in, and with some running (l-h) Side, getting position on Black; (3) a fine cut, without Side, to get on Black; (4) a very fine cut at an angle, fast pace being necessary; the c-b would proceed up the table in the direction shown by the arrow; (5) $\frac{1}{4}$-b cut; (6) cutting Blue in with Bottom and some r-h side, to slow up c-b's pace, and to get position on the red (6); (7) cut on Black, leaving it safe, c-b travelling to the bottom end. It helps, in fine cuts, to get down as low as possible. Note that in all diagrams of Cuts and thin contacts, it is the edge of the c-b that contacts the o-b, as indicated in D.15, No. 4. I have, however, adopted the usual way of representing such strokes.

POTTING BALLS TOUCHING THE CUSHION

When the o-b lies touching a cushion, as in D.16, stroke 1, by striking the cushion a split second, so to speak, before the o-b—it amounts to a practically simultaneous contact of ball and cushion—and using some running Side (here r-h), the pot can be made without difficulty; pace must not be fast. Some theorists declare this to be a case of "transmitted" Side, i.e. they declare the r-h side imparts l-h side, which means pocket Side in this stroke, but few support this theory. Provided the contact is right, the o-b *must* enter the pocket, as it contacts the farther jaw, and, as a matter of fact, the pot can be made (with accurate contact) without any Side being applied to the c-b. The use of running Side in this stroke is a matter of controversy. That it helps is proved by its efficacy and almost general use. Its probable function is that it brings the c-b on to correct (and full) contact with the o-b should the c-b strike the cushion prematurely, and it helps to achieve the

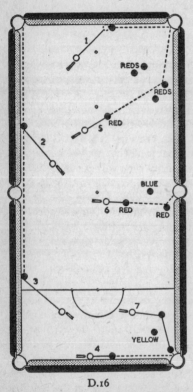

D.16

same kind of position or contact on the o-b as if we were potting with the c-b also touching the cushion; i.e. its sharp throw-off from the cushion places the latter directly behind the o-b. The aim in this pot is not easy, as is obvious. As the stroke resembles a Cut, and the finest of Cuts at that, it may help to treat the stroke as such. Or, if we imagine a line through the centre of the o-b running parallel with the cushion (as shown—it is, of course, the path of the potted ball), we must contact the point at which this line protrudes on its nearer side. Or, again, imagine the c-b to be lying next to (i.e. touching) the red; we then seek to displace the imaginary c-b with the actual one. These hints are, of course, theoretical, and, in practice, we shall find that we soon develop the knack of simultaneous striking of cushion and o-b. When the c-b is also actually touching the cushion, as in stroke 4, the stroke is difficult, and only possible at slow pace. Dead accurate contact is indispensable and, of course, no Side is needed. In such a position the actual pot is all that may be hoped for, as any attempt to gain position by pace will impair the accurate striking necessary for the pot. Reverting to stroke 1, this pot is "on" even in the positions 2 and 3; (3) is, of course, a mere speculation, but it is worth trying as a "shot to nothing" (see D.19), if the state of the game permits.

INDIRECT AND CANNON POTS

D.16: Nos. 5 and 6 show the indirect pot; (5) we clearly cannot pot any of the four reds shown, but we may effect a pot-red by directing the nearest red on to the farthest, as shown; (6) a similar stroke; (7) Yellow obstructs a direct stroke on to the red near the pocket; by cannoning off the other red we pot the latter, using strong Bottom to prevent the c-b following into the pocket, should we contact the red in a line with the pocket.

PLANTS AND SETS

Strictly speaking, a "Plant" is a position in which two balls
are touching in the vicinity of a pocket, and in such a way that
a line drawn through their centres is at a right angle to one

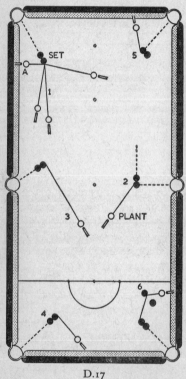

drawn from the pocket
centre to the centre of
the ball we can pot
(D.17, No. 2), whereas
a "Set" occurs when
two balls are touching,
as in a Plant, but in
such a position that a
line drawn through
their centres leads to
the pocket (D.17, No.
1). Nowadays, no such
differentiation is made,
and the terms, Plant
and Set, are used indis-
criminately. In stroke
1, D.17 (Set), provided
the outer ball be struck
on its point farthest
from the pocket, or as
near to it as possible, the
inside ball will enter the
pocket even from *A*. In
stroke 2, D.17, the ball
to be potted is struck,
instead of the second
ball, as in stroke 1, a
thin contact, on the side farther from the pocket, serving to
pot the ball in such a position. Sets, as we will call them, are
not automatic; they can fail, but in the majority of instances

D.17

they succeed. In stroke 1, for instance, it is obvious that as the balls are in a straight line, any impetus given to the outside ball on its near side must communicate itself to the inside one, and cause it to enter the pocket. Stroke 2 is not quite so theoretically sure, but invariably the same thing happens, although here, of course, if the ball be struck as we should strike it if no other ball were touching it, it must enter the pocket. A full ball must not be made. Nos. 3 and 5 need fair pace.

Often when, in the type of stroke 1, the balls are not quite straight, the pot can be made. D.18 shows a "fancy" Set, which some professionals include in trick shot exhibitions. The two balls (No. 1) are not in a line with the pocket, a line through

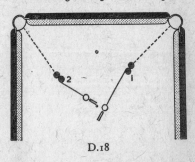

D.18

their centres leading to a point 3 or 4 in. from it (to the left). To pot the ball nearer the pocket one would assume that one would have to contact the first ball *on its right*, in order to counter the fact that the straight line through their centres leads to the *left* of the pocket, but the reverse method is the solution, i.e. we contact it (rather thinly) on its left side. No. 2 is a similar stroke. The stroke is something of a paradox, the explanation probably lying in what takes place when the middle ball is sandwiched. A "hidden" Set occurs when the ball to be struck is obstructed by another ball. See stroke 6 (D.17). Here we cannon off another red to effect the Set pot. There are countless Set positions, strokes 3, 4 and 5 (D.17) being examples. Often a good Set occurs in the early stages when the Pack is partially broken and a number of reds are still touching. By going up the table and having a look, such Sets may be detected. If we spot one we may then employ the "Shot to nothing" (see D.19), in exploiting such a Set.

THE "SHOT TO NOTHING"

A most valuable stroke. Often we find ourselves with nothing at all certain to pot when the c-b lies in the bottom area of the table, yet in the region of the top quarter there may be a red

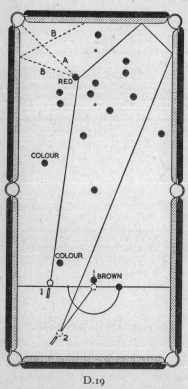

D.19

or a colour (whichever we are "on") for which a clear path to a pocket exists. Our primary purpose is to return to the Baulk area, of course. If, therefore, we combine two objects, viz. returning to the "safe" area and making speculative contact on the ball which is thus pottable, with a view to potting it, we make the "shot to nothing", so called because we may fail to make the pot, yet incur no risk as we bring the c-b back to safety, just as we would if no such pot were attempted. The stroke resembles the opening one at the start of the game, but it has the advantage that if we pot the ball (a red, invariably, as colours are rarely to be found so situated) we shall have the chance to effect a "red-hot" snooker behind a "Baulk" colour. We must ensure, of course, that we have a clear run to Baulk should we fail to pot the ball. D.19 shows an example. We notice the red (named) is "on", so perform the "shot to nothing". If we pot the red (line A), by stroke 2 we can snooker behind Brown by a gentle and very slow stroke.

If we fail to pot the red the latter will run safe (line B) and we remain near the bottom cushion, as depicted. Whether, therefore, we pot the red or not, we have risked "nothing", except an in-off which, of course, we must guard against.

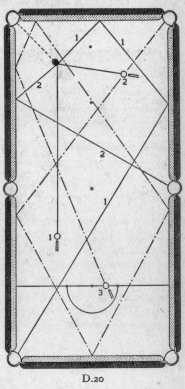

D.20

ANGLES

It is advisable to acquire a reliable knowledge of table angles as many all-round strokes are necessary in Snooker; by "all round" I mean strokes which involve contact of the c-b with two, three or more cushions, and those which, like doubles, include cross-table or "round the corner" strokes. Many of the penalties given away in Snooker are due to the c-b's going in-off, and this often occurs in the "shot to nothing" stroke, and in defensive strokes, off a ball lying in the top area, back into the bottom section of the table. Whenever we pot a ball at any speed, therefore, we should visualize the path the c-b must take, so as to vary the contact or apply a little Side in order to avoid going in-off, knocking another ball in, etc., if such a mishap appears likely. D.20: strokes 1 and 2 illustrate an in-off after potting of the red ball, and will enable the reader to take such a possibility into account when making other pots which involve the c-b's travelling round corners or across the table. Stroke 3 (dash-and-dot line) shows a five-cushion stroke round the table (first cushion contact about 6 in. below the Spot), and it will be seen that this stroke causes the c-b to contact the bottom cushion near its centre, also that, by varying the contact on the first cushion struck, the course of the c-b may be changed accordingly, that is, contact on the cushions may be made farther on or nearer, as the case may require. The best way of becoming familiar with these angles of incidence (on to) and reflection (off the cushion) is by way of experiment and observation, so the reader should place his c-b in the "D" and, playing from the Spots and half-way between the Centre and End Spots, in succession, note the various courses of the c-b, in plain-ball striking and with r-h and l-h side, as he aims to contact the top side cushion at different places. Knowing the angular contacts of the table is invaluable for getting out of snookers, as it is at Billiards for making all-round cannons, and practice will repay the labour involved. Stroke 3, by the way, needs ample running (here r-h) Side, as running Side results in a livelier throw-off from the cushion (it is probably called "running" for this reason) whereas check Side acts as a brake on the speed of the cushion throw-off.

BREAK-MAKING AND TACTICS

Breaks, of course, are very important in match-winning Snooker, but they are something of a will-o'-the-wisp if the player makes them the primary objective, for it is tactics which, given players of more or less equal calibre generally, win, and often, too, against superior players. The player who makes the highest breaks does not necessarily beat his rivals. Often a series of small items, such as 9, 6, 11, 18 and so on, wins the frame, if accompanied by clever tactics. Naturally, if a player makes, say, a 40-odd break in the early stages, he is more than half-way to winning the frame, and a player whose positional play is good enough, given good openings, to make 40s and 50s will prove a very hard man to beat. Nevertheless, his very skill in break-making may often cause him to take risks to keep the break going, and so, missing, as he may easily do, a difficult stroke, let his opponent in frequently. Many games have been seen in the Amateur Championship in which the better break-maker has been beaten by good tactics, which did not give him the chances to make a big break. Against this, however, is the equally significant fact that, *if* the player, able to make a big break, is also a good tactician, then he will be the hardest player to beat, for he will be doubly equipped. Consequently, the art of break-making, coupled with an astute tactical sense, constitutes the complete Snooker player.

The objective, of course, is *winning*, not making breaks, and, as stated above, the gifted break-maker is often apt to forget this, and, in his anxiety to make a big break (a 100-break, of course, is the magnet to such a player) he is often apt to forget he is playing to win, and not to beat his personal record, or perhaps the record in the particular competition concerned. A big break at Snooker naturally wins loud applause, whereas winning the frame is, of course, greeted with applause, but not so demonstrative.

Playing to win, therefore, means making a judicial tactical (defensive) stroke directly good position is lost, instead of trying to keep the break going. If, however, position is *not* lost, and the next pot does *not* involve undue risk, then, of course, it is the game to try to continue the break. Naturally, if a player has reached 50 or 60 in a break, risks may be taken as it is invariably a frame-winning score, when made early on or in the middle stages of the frame, but a 50-break right at the start does not by any means automatically spell victory, as the reds left are still ample for the other player to win.

The secret of break-making is, of course, ball control, as at Billiards. Potting becomes, for the first-class player, more or less automatic and subsidiary to position. Many young players think it is possible to learn some magical secret or other, enabling them to make rapid strides in mastery of the game, but only hard practice and true cueing will bring improvement, and it will be gradual not sudden. The "fundamentals" (stance, the bridge, delivery, etc.) must, therefore, be checked from time to time, particularly if results are not favourable, and one-ball practice is a certain check. If you can consistently make the c-b return over the Spots on a straight line or near to it, your cueing will be all that is needed.

Naturally the Black ball is the basis of break-making for it lies near two pockets, and as the red balls are generally, for most of the game, in its vicinity, it is obvious that sequences of reds and Black are possible in conjunction with the two top-pkts, and that this sequence cannot be excelled or equalled by any other combined process on the table. To familiarize oneself with the principle and technique of red-and-Black play, the Spot Stroke and the Top-of-the-table game (at Billiards) are invaluable, particularly the former, which, as it includes no cannons, is especially suited for the non-Billiards-playing Snooker player.

The player must not, of course, make a fetish of the Black, as a profitable sequence can often be executed with Blue or with Pink, but continuity is not possible to the same degree with these balls, and reds are not likely to be available in such quantity as with Black. Nevertheless, it is often the game, in potting a red into a top-pkt, to come back off the top cushion to get on Blue, and not to stay on Black, as the latter stroke may bring complications involving either a slow stroke, which is often dangerous, as the c-b may roll off or we may easily miss at slow pace, or we may be snatching at 7 points (a dubious shadow) for a substantial bone, namely, a certain Blue. As I have said already, when we pot a ball, position is all-important. Therefore, we must pot it in the right way to obtain position, and not just the right way to achieve the pot. We may be able to pot the ball by a plain stroke, but maybe a plain stroke will not secure position, but only a Stun or Screw or Follow-on stroke. In potting, therefore, we must take this into account, not only foreseeing a pot but also how that pot will have to be made. The problem is to attain precision in both potting and position, and this is the art of Snooker at its pinnacle. During a break one should make a survey of the position, as it develops, and try to foresee which balls will lead to its continuance and which to its ending. Mastery of positional play, of course, makes each pot easier than it would be without such mastery so that we can continue our break much longer, but until we have reached advanced skill in break-building, and even when we have, it will be unwise to forget that we are playing to win, and not to make breaks. There will be many situations in which a tactical stroke will be much more profitable than venturing on a pot which involves undue risk. As I have indicated, even first-class players bear this in mind, and in championship play, even in the Professional World Championship, breaks are invariably much smaller than in exhibition matches, the players avoiding undue risks. Snookering is, in important games, an integral part of tactics, and its advantages must never be forgotten. A really good snooker, moreover, is not just a defensive stroke but, in essence, an attacking one, for it leads to an opening. Whenever, therefore, the chance of a good snooker occurs, take it: it may be a match winner, and, at the least, it will give what is all-important, the initiative.

In the early stages of a frame opportunities for snookering occur in the return to the Baulk area, and these often determine the result of it. Opportunities of breaking the pack, without risk, should be taken. And do not forget to develop the art of "thinking ahead"! The Black, for instance, may be "on" but continuance of the break may be hindered, not helped, by potting it, and you will often see the skilled player take the Yellow or the Green, for example, instead of an easy

Black which will only take him off the natural path of the
break. The importance of looking ahead cannot, therefore, be
too heavily stressed. Getting position on a ball does not mean
just getting to a spot whence it may be potted, but getting to
one from which it may be potted and *position on the next ball*
obtained. When, for example, you are on the last red and near
the Black, you will have to consider whether, if you pot the
red to get on the Black, for the 7 points, should you need them,
you will be able, after potting the Black, to get position on the
Yellow at the other end. Always pot a ball with a purpose, as
it were, and not just to get the points. Also, it is often possible,
in potting a ball, to improve the position of one badly placed.

TAKING THE COLOURS

Often, for they will have been re-spotted more than once,
the colours are found on their spots when it comes to potting
the last red. To "take the colours" is to pot the six balls,
whether on their Spots or not, in their proper sequence. After
potting the last red, one has, of course, a colour at disposal, and
this potted, we are on the Yellow. If the colour we choose,
after the last red, is the Yellow, then it is re-spotted, and we
begin to take the colours by potting it again. Which colour we
may choose after this last red depends, of course, on the situation, as, when potting this colour, we must have the Yellow in
view. Taking the colours does not follow a stereotyped formula,
for the simple reason that any of the six balls may require a
different type of stroke to pot it; that is, a Stun, Screw,
Follow-through or plain-ball one, and any of these may require
contact with one or more cushions. All one can do is to show
one way of "taking the colours", see D.21. Stroke 1: Yellow
is potted by a screw-back stroke, to get on Green (2), and, also,
at the proper angle to get on Brown next. Thus, in potting
each ball, we have to bear in mind that the shortest way to
each colour is by positional accuracy. Green is potted, again
with a soft Screw Stroke to 3, and Brown by a stroke, with

running Side, off the side cushion to take Blue next. In obtaining position on Blue, we must keep on the lower side of it; otherwise we shall have to send the c-b round the bottom-end of the table to get on Pink. Getting on the lower side of Blue must often be done in a break in order to get to the top-end. We pot Blue by a follow-through (or run-through) stroke with a little check (r-h) Side to keep to the right of Pink, and Pink, by a Screw shot, which leaves us in good position on Black, for a plain-ball pot. When you have become proficient in Stun, Screw, Follow-through Strokes, and can use Side efficiently, you will be able to select which type of stroke is necessary to pot a particular colour. "Clearing the table" may mean "taking the colours" alone, or potting all the balls at any stage of a frame.

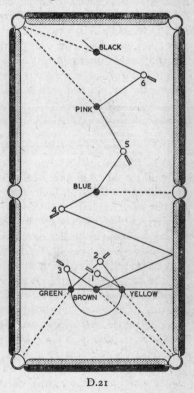

D.21

Colours, as I have said, should be selected for their positional advantages, and not for their numerical value. Often a low-value colour is the way to the break, and potting the Black or Pink a blind alley. This ability to judge the situation from a break-making standpoint instead of as a mere additional number of points, is one of the most valuable in the game. In the early stages no chance of breaking the pack should be missed but it is vital that the stroke so breaking it should not itself be missed. The "shot to nothing" (D.19) is an invaluable asset in forcing openings; it will, therefore, be useful to put red balls up in the vicinity of, and to the side of, the

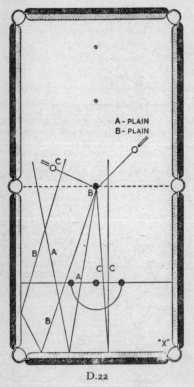

A - PLAIN
B - PLAIN

D.22

Pyramid Spot, i.e. a circular area of about a 2-ft. radius, and practise potting them from, and near, the "D", as this is the region in which the o-b lies for the "shot to nothing".

A stroke which must be mastered thoroughly is that whereby the Blue is potted into a centre-pkt from a position above its Spot. D.22 shows this stroke. Unless we are on a bot-pkt red, next stroke after potting the Blue, the c-b has to be brought back again to the centre and top where reds are available. In this stroke, firstly, collision with the three bottom colours has to be avoided, and secondly, we have to consider whether this can be done by a plain stroke, possibly off a side cushion as well as the bottom, or a Screw stroke. D.22: Stroke A indicates the plain stroke off the bottom cushion; B, the plain stroke off the bottom and side cushions, necessary if the c-b were half the distance from the dotted line; C position needs a Screw stroke, with slight check (here r-h)

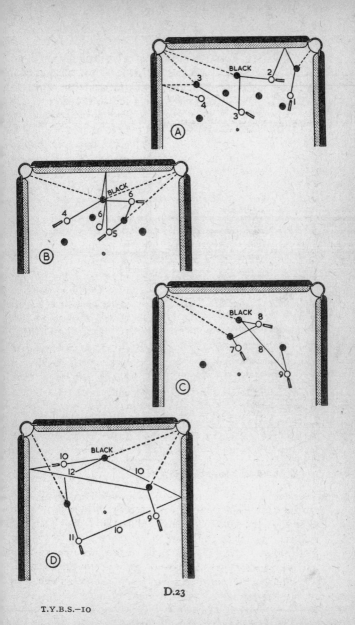

Side, to prevent Yellow being hit on the rebound off the bottom cushion. Were this stroke played as a plain-ball one (like *A* and *B*) the c-b would probably go into the r-h bot-pkt, "*X*". Here again there is a variation, as we may have to direct the c-b *outside* the Yellow, off the bottom cushion, and again it depends on the position of the c-b. These strokes will, however, initiate the reader into the two ways of potting the Blue by a plain stroke (*A* and *B*) or by Screw, with check Side (*C*).

D.23: *A*, *B*, *C* and *D* illustrate a red-Black sequence, totalling 48 points, 6 reds, 6 Blacks.

A: Red potted into top-pkt, with Bottom (to check pace) and a little check Side, to keep away from Black (plain h-b would bring c-b too near Black; (2) Black potted by soft Screw stroke to get on No. 3 red, which is itself potted by partial run-through to rebound off cushion, a little check (r-h) Side is used to get c-b as straight as possible on Black, but as seen we have not used enough, nevertheless, we are well on Black. *B*: We pot Black (stroke 4) and with a follow-through stroke, and some check Side, to come straight off cushion, for position on red (stroke 5); (5) red is potted by gentle run-through, plain ball, Black (stroke 6) is potted by Screw stroke for position on red, as shown. *C*: We pot the next red (stroke 7) by a soft screw-back shot to pot Black again (stroke 8); we now make a very strong screw-back stroke off Black, for position on the red near the r-h cushion (stroke 9). *D*: We pot this red (stroke 9) with a Screw Stun stroke, sending the c-b across the table for potting Black, after it rebounds off cushion; (10) pot Black, to come off far cushion for position on last red, which we pot (stroke 11) with a run-through shot and then we can pot Black again, having scored 48 points in 12 strokes. Some of these pots could, of course, be done in another way (No. 9, for example, could be made by a plain-ball stroke, to get on Black off the top and l-h side cushions) but this applies to all breaks, such is the variety of means whereby strokes can be performed. Stroke 8, potting Black, could also be made by a run-through stroke, with running (l-h) Side, to come off the opposite cushion to get on red for stroke 9. Often pots may be made in various ways, positional considerations deciding the matter.

POTENTIALITIES OF THE COLOURS

The Black, as stated before, is the most lucrative ball in conjunction with the reds, and, as, for instance, with only three of the latter, a 24-break can be made, its rewarding power is obvious. Black exploitation is, furthermore, favoured by the comparatively small area it calls for, and also by the three-cushion contacts it offers, similarly to the Top-of-the-table game. Naturally it demands skill of a delicate order. Nevertheless, positional play always governs the situation and, therefore, the Black ball should never be played on unless its use fits in with that requirement. Players often try to stay on the Black when potting a long red, which, as a rule, is, of course, mistaken and dangerous, as, if the red is missed, and long pots often are missed, your opponent is on velvet. Blue, being centrally situated, is a valuable ball, as it is often easy to get on it after potting a red in a top-pkt or bot-pkt, not to mention the mid-pkts. Blue provides often a "sparsely populated" area, affording thus good scope for manœuvring. Sometimes we can pot the Blue, using the top or top and side cushions in the same way as that shown in D.22, where we pot it and bring the c-b away off the bottom or bottom and side cushions. We can also often cut the Blue in and come back from either the top or bottom area to the central. The Pink is most useful when a few reds are near it, but not obstructing each other, for then we have four pockets to work on, and by (mainly) Stun or Screw strokes a nice sequence is possible. The three bottom colours have their uses when reds are near them; otherwise they seem, until the game is well advanced, almost to serve as well for snookering as for potting. After potting a red into a bot-pkt, we can often, by a stun pot, pot one of these bottom colours into a centre-pkt, or even a top-pkt if the coast is clear, and thus keep the c-b in the Baulk area. It is, however, risky, after potting a red into a bot-pkt, to attempt a colour pot into a mid-pkt by a follow-through stroke or a slow-paced one, for the pot will often be at an awkward angle, and if it is missed we shall have left the c-b high up the table and ideally placed for our opponent.

TACTICS AGAIN

The best tactics to pursue depend on one's special gifts, style of play, and, of course, on our opponent. If one is a first-class potter, then an adventurous policy, though not, of course, a reckless one, for reckless players, however brilliant, are asking for trouble, will be good tactics. If one's strong point is c-b control, and one's potting is not exceptional or distinctive in itself, then tying up our opponent by astute tactical moves will serve best. Undoubtedly the best policy for a player who pots well, and is also skilled in ball control, is to try the pot whenever a reasonable opportunity exists, and to snooker or play strategically when the state of the game demands it. The good player's policy should be suited to his opponent's ability and the state of the game. Attack and defence can both be overdone. The important thing is to develop skill at both, and to call each into requisition as needed. The player who keeps sending the c-b back to the bottom area and only pots the "certainty" will not win many games, and will, almost surely, weary all concerned, opponent and spectators. Nevertheless, Snooker is the name of the game, and those who, whether players or spectators, look upon it as timid, as some do, are unmindful of the fact that, as I have previously stressed, it is, if skilful, a means of attack, bringing openings and the initiative. To make Snooker a potting picnic or orgy is to lower the game. I have seen many a frame won by an adventurous pot which has brought a good break, but also many a frame won by a couple of perfect snookers. The ideal policy, therefore, is to pot when a pot is reasonably "on"; to try for the pot (even if difficult) if you can provide for a safe position of the c-b should you miss, and if the chance of a snooker occurs which will make your opponent play blind up the table, to lay a snooker.

The snooker, of course, becomes of paramount importance when a player is behind by more than the value of the balls left on the table. It is obvious that it is easier to snooker while all these balls are left. It is, therefore, best to try to lay the snooker or snookers while the "going is good", but many players delay too long in potting balls in such a situation in the attempt to snooker, with the result that the opponent pots them, and his task is made all the harder and perhaps impossible. So if, in such a situation, that is, one in which only the colours are left, and one or two snookers are needed to win, you find it possible to take the Yellow and Green, and even Brown, it is advisable to do so. Three balls (Blue, Pink and Black) are ample for snookering. The good Snooker player, therefore, is neither the all-out attacker nor the "stonewaller", but the one who adapts his tactics to the situation and the opponent. Indulgence in a purely defensive role over a long period has the effect of upsetting the potting mechanism, as it were. This is why, even in professional games, a player, though certain to lose the frame, tries to make it as difficult as he can for his opponent to pot the last three or four balls, as, by so doing, he is, as it were, throwing his opponent out of his potting stride for the next frame. He does this, of course, by continuing to send the ball "on" into a safe position, and his opponent's answer is to send the ball "on" gently towards a pocket in order to pot it, if possible, and to leave it in the jaws, if he does not, so that the other player will find it difficult to keep it out of the pocket. Personally, I think the best answer to this thwarting policy is to make a vigorous Stun Stroke, to pot the ball, if possible, and should the pot fail, your Stun Stroke will have sent the o-b careering round the table, and so possibly cause it to enter another pocket. As you will have stunned the c-b, no danger of an in-off exists. I have not seen this policy adopted, however, but it seems preferable to me to that of rolling the o-b gently towards a pocket, and thus prolonging the agony, even if it is just trusting to luck.

GETTING OUT OF A SNOOKER

Getting out of a snooker is worth a little study. The table angles should, of course, be learned. Contacting the snookered ball is in some instances just a matter of luck, but, if it is at all possible, care should be taken to make a calculated, and not a mere happy-go-lucky stroke. Whether one's stroke is a slow or fast one depends, of course, on the position. Often a stroke, calculated just to contact the ball which is snookered, will ensure safe position, and even snooker one's opponent, but this, of course, is a matter of luck, although it does, in fact, proceed from a stroke intended to bring about such a result. D.24 shows a case. The player is snookered on the red by Blue, Black and Pink. Playing a rather slow stroke, he contacts the ball "on" (red), and the c-b pushes the latter through the gap, and itself finishes behind the Pink, thus snookering the player who laid the snooker. A fast shot here would be folly. The cushions have often to be struck directly when getting out of a

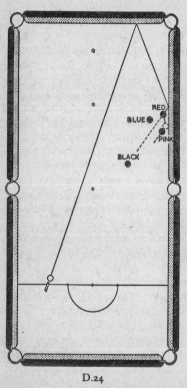

D.24

snooker, so the player should make a point of practising cushion-first strokes at all angles, remembering that the point of
contact, at a sharp angle (i.e. diagonal), is always half a ball in
advance of the point of aim.

Situations often occur, when the table is fairly crowded, in
which the way for a return stroke to the bottom area is barred.
It is often possible in such a position to run through a ball
by a $\frac{3}{4}$-b contact on to the top cushion, either directly or via
the side cushion, provided no reds are near the top pockets for
our opponent to take. In that case we should, as a last resource,
have to play a vigorous forcing stroke in the hope of getting
back somehow.

THE DELIBERATE OR "INTENTIONAL" MISS

An unfair player, or even a habitually fair one, momentarily
tempted, if faced with a position at Snooker in which, after
having been "snookered", it appears to him more advantageous to miss the ball "on" than to (try seriously to) contact
it, as the Rules oblige him to do, may decide to miss it, while
pretending to hit it. If the referee thinks such a miss deliberate,
he may request the player to replay the stroke if the balls are
replaceable; if not, however, he may ask the offending player
to take the next stroke. If the player repeats the miss, and it is
again adjudged intentional by the referee, the latter may dis-
qualify him.

General Rule 15. This important rule is not commonly
known or taken into consideration. It enjoins upon the referee,
amongst other things, to be "careful to see that a player is not
better off by reason of a contravention of the Rules than he
would be by their strict observance". This applies to both
games. Example: A player fouls at Snooker, and his foul
stroke sends the c-b into the pile of reds, making it very
difficult for his opponent to take his stroke. The referee, under
General Rule 15, has power to rectify such a handicap by
placing the c-b in a playable position, taking care, of course,
not to present him with a gift pot.

NOTE
TO THIS IMPRESSION

Since *Teach Yourself Billiards and Snooker* was published in 1957 a few alterations have been made in the Official Rules of the two games. The following ones should be noted:

Billiards

Rule 7. Consecutive cannons are still limited to 35 but, on the completion of this number, the break may be continued only by the intervention of a winning or losing hazard, or a cannon in conjunction with a hazard. Previously, a hazard or indirect cannon, or direct cannon in conjunction with a hazard, was the means by which the break could continue.

Snooker

An important amendment to Rule 14 concerns contravention of the Rules. Formerly, General Rule 15 laid upon the referee the duty of seeing that a player did not benefit by a foul stroke. The amendment to Rule 14, passed on January 8th, 1958, relieves him of this obligation. The rule may be phrased as follows: After a foul stroke by his opponent, a player may, (1) play from the position left; (2) claim a free ball (or "nominated" ball, as it is called in the rules), if he is snookered by the foul, or (3) request his opponent to take the next stroke.

Regarding No. 3, if the opponent, when complying with such request, fouls a second time, he may again be asked to take the next stroke, and, in fact, as many times as he commits a foul, but, even two successive foul strokes are rare. As to No. 2, the non-offender need not take the free ball unless he so desires.

An important change in the rule governing "spotting the Black" was introduced, and this is fully explained in Rule 8.

As stated in the Note (p. vi), which follows the Foreword, the reader is advised to procure a copy of the rules of billiards and snooker, which, for the reason given in the Note referred to, cannot be embodied in this book.

One official decision, which concerns both games, was that of banning the "Jump Shot" (see p. 200) in 1958, the official definition of the stroke reading: "A stroke in which the cue-ball is made to jump over an intervening ball", that is, intervening between the cue-ball and the ball the player is intending to strike.

Nomination

As many players are not clear about the rule of "nominating", it may be useful to clarify a point or two. Awarded a free (i.e. nominated) ball *after a foul stroke by his opponent*, a player is *obliged* to nominate or declare which colour he intends to play. If there has been no foul he need not nominate, provided it is obvious to the referee which ball he has in mind to play at. It may happen, however, that two or more colours lie close together and in such a case the referee might well be uncertain.

Note on Diagram 6 (Billiards, p. 20)

Stroke 5. A losing hazard, with the o-b on the Pyramid Spot, is rare but, frequent when it is in the immediate vicinity. In the diagram the stroke is shown as a guide only for the latter contingency. Owing, how, to lack of room, it was not possible to feature the actual stroke. Given a ball on the Pyramid Spot, the c-b must be spotted in the "D", 3 to 4 inches from the end of the "D" line, *but* the losing hazard must be made into the opposite top pocket, that is, spotting on the right-hand side of the "D", the aim must be at the left-hand top pocket and vice-versa.

Stroke 1 (D.6). The "long loser", with the o-b on the Centre Spot. I stated that spotting the c-b should be made "about 6 in. from the Baulk-line". The reason for this is the advisability of "equalising" as much as possible the distance between the c-b and the o-b and that between the latter and the top pocket. The reader is advised to spot for this stroke (as stated, a basic one of billiards) some $3\frac{1}{2}$ in. from the end of the "D" line (i.e. from the right- or left-hand Spot) and then as stated (see p. 21), take the c-b back some 6 in. or more.

GENERAL

THE "PUSH" STROKE

This is forbidden by the Rules ("the ball must be struck, not pushed") but not defined. To "push" is to make a stroke in which the cue remains on the c-b longer than the term "to strike" connotes, and the resultant effect resembles pushing the ball. To strike the c-b twice in a rapid manner is also a push. The foul gener-ally occurs when the c-b is nearly touching the o-b, and the cue impact, the cue remaining on the c-b, causes the cue, c-b and o-b to be "locked" together for a moment or two. The only ways the push can be avoided are (see D.25): (1) to make a Massé stroke; (2) to strike the top of the c-b forward (in follow-through fashion) so that the cue glances off the top: this can be done by the skilled player in a position when it is desired to run-through the first o-b, but it needs very deft cuemanship;

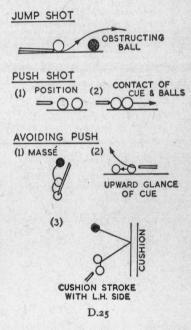

JUMP SHOT

OBSTRUCTING BALL

PUSH SHOT
(1) POSITION   (2) CONTACT OF CUE & BALLS

AVOIDING PUSH
(1) MASSÉ   (2)

UPWARD GLANCE OF CUE

(3)

CUSHION

CUSHION STROKE WITH L.H. SIDE

D.25

(3) to go round the o-b by a glancing stroke with Side, if needed, as shown in D.25(3). Here a good player could run-through the first o-b if the red were clear of a kiss, but when the c-b and first o-b are almost touching, a push, even with a good player, is inevitable except by a glancing stroke, as shown.

THE JUMP SHOT

Many people, myself included, think the jump shot (D.25) should be barred. If the ball "on" is obstructed by another ball, say about 6 in. in front of the c-b, we can cause the latter to "jump over" the intervening ball, by laying the cue on the cloth about 2 in. in front of the c-b and striking its underneath part after a short backward movement, the cue trailing on the cloth during the entire stroke. Fair strength is needed. A low or flat bridge is necessary so that the cue gets as near the table bed as possible. If the stroke is attempted by a downward cut or stab, the cloth may be cut, which is why hall proprietors often bar it. The stroke savours rather of the "trick" variety, but it is permitted by the Rules. One well-known player labelled it, disparagingly, "aerial Billiards". At the time of writing, the Jump Shot (one in which the cue-ball is made to jump over an intervening ball, whether by design or accident) has just been officially declared to be a foul.

THE RESTS

The rest is an implement to enable us to play strokes when the c-b is too far away to reach with the normal bridge. The short rest is for such a stroke at about 5 or 6 ft. distance; the half-butt for strokes three-quarters of the length of the table away, and the long rest for the extreme distance possible. There are long cues, to match, for the half-butt and the long rest.

The short rest is most in demand. It should be laid flat and firm on the table, with the cue tip, as much as possible, in alignment with it, the tip about 12 to 15 in. from the c-b. In some positions, in which other balls obstruct, cue and rest must be held diagonally. The cue, the tip end of which slides along the rest bridge, a cross, should be held with the thumb and the first two fingers. Some players hold the rest fairly straight, others rather to the left of the body. If straight, i.e. in alignment with the cue, sighting or aiming should be about under the chin. Checking the distance with one's cue shows whether we need the rest. The player who, if right-handed, can play certain strokes (which need the rest) with the left hand can dispense with the rest in a great many instances (and, of course, the left-hander can do likewise with his right hand). Do not raise the butt of the cue too high, the nearer to the cue height we employ when we play normally (i.e. without the rest), the better. Placing the rest with its cross-head low is best for the majority of strokes (✕); placing it thus (✗) serves for strokes that need a higher bridge. Practice is invaluable for using the rest well, as many a break comes to an end owing to careless or faulty use of the rest. My advice is: never shirk getting the rest; so many can't be bothered. The long rests are used in the same way, but it should be borne in mind that there is so much timber in them that the extra weight imparts strong force by itself to the stroke, and this should be allowed for.

THE SPIDER

This is a sort of extra high rest to enable us to strike the c-b when another ball or balls lie so near, perhaps touching it, as to make (tip) contact with it very difficult and awkward. It is used more in Snooker than in Billiards. By adjusting it in such a way that you are able to strike the c-b over the obstructing ball or balls (though perhaps only on its upper surface) you are able to make your stroke. Place the spider as near to the obstructing ball(s) as possible, raise your cue and strike very carefully. It is easy to foul a ball, or miscue on the c-b. Also, beware of fouling a ball or balls when removing the rest or spider.

CUES

A cue of one's own is indispensable. Cues differ enormously, and getting the ideal one is not easy. Weight and balance are all important, but as the Professional Billiards Championship has been won by a player using a 21-oz. cue and by one using a cue of $15\frac{1}{2}$ oz., and as $16\frac{1}{2}$ oz. is considered the ideal for Snooker, and 17 or 18 oz. for Billiards, it is obvious the matter needs thought. I think the best cue, however, is one which feels as though it were part of your physique when you handle it, that is, you should feel entirely comfortable with it. It is a good plan to sample the various cues in a billiard-hall and thus find out, by making a few shots with each, what weight shape and length suits you. You will thus, when purchasing one, know exactly what type of cue you find suits you in every respect. The regulation length is 4 ft. 10 in., the favourite weights, 17 or 18 oz. Nevertheless, you may find a shorter cue or a lighter or heavier one more to your liking. The extra weight helps in Stun, Screw and forcing strokes. Ideally, one should have different cues for different strokes, as in golf, but as you cannot change your cue half a dozen times every moment or two this is impossible.

In a good cue the grain should run straight and be quite smooth, and the cue should be flexible and stiff; avoid a whippy cue at all costs. Balance should be perfect as you hold it, that is, a few inches from the end. Length should be in proportion to one's height and reach. The tip should be about 11 mm.; some players like a 10-mm. tip. A small tip is not, in my view, advisable. Some cues have the same thickness for about 12 to 15 in. from the tip; some increase gradually in thickness from the tip; I think the latter kind are preferable from the point of view of stiffness.

Every good player carries and keeps his cue in a special case. Treat your cue tenderly, that is, do not bang it on the floor or drop it; to clean it use a damp cloth, and then rub linseed oil into it with the palm of the hand, drying it with brown paper. Do not use sand-paper.

Once you possess a good cue, never stand it against the wall, but keep it in a cue-case, which you should acquire, or, until you have one, lay it on a flat surface, such as the floor, a long table or shelf, otherwise it will warp.

Tipping a Cue

This is really a job for an expert, and information may easily be obtained from one, or from the firm selling the cue. Special glue may be had from Billiard firms with which to stick the tip on. The tip surface should be made perfectly level (i.e. clear of bits of the glue from previous tipping); a file may be used for this. The surface of the tip is then smeared thinly with the glue, which should have been warmed, and the new tip applied, and pressed down (by upending the cue on the floor), care being taken to see that the tip does not overlap the edges of the cue at any point. Stand the cue upside down (on its tip) and leave overnight in a perpendicular position. Tips are also (and mostly) put on by means of a wafer; this way, however, is rather intricate, and needs experience. Until you get experience in tipping cues, you should have recourse either to a Billiard firm or an experienced marker, steward or player, who will readily help you. Most players nowadays have a metal ferrule fixed to the end of their cues. This keeps the cue from splitting, dispenses with filing and cutting when affixing a new tip, and protects the tip-end very effectively. It is possible to acquire interchangeable tips. A metal holder takes the tip and is screwed on to the cue. Refills are obtainable, so that if the tip gets damaged, one can immediately be fitted to the cue. As, in the 1956 Amateur Snooker Championship, a player's tip came off when he was leading by a good margin, so that he needed to borrow a cue for the next session (in which he lost all five frames), the advantage of this interchangeable tip is obvious. I strongly recommend it.

PSYCHOLOGICAL

Vital Aids in Both Games

Concentration

One of the most important things in both Billiards and Snooker, particularly the former, because of the much longer stays at the table—a break of 100 may occupy seven or eight minutes—is *concentration*. Countless strokes are missed and countless breaks come to an end through the player's concentration lapsing. The technical point or points involved in every stroke must grip the attention so that the player keeps prominent in mind and purpose what he has to do in that particular stroke. It is well, therefore, that every player should school himself to putting up with every kind of disturbing noise or influence which is apt to crop up in the billiard hall, and this means that he should accept them as inevitable and bound to occur, instead of allowing irritation to ruffle him and disturb his fixity of purpose. In cultivating the gift of concentration, therefore, he should welcome such things when they occur in ordinary games, as, by doing so, he will train himself to be unruffled or annoyed by them should they occur in serious matches. Everything must be excluded from the mind but the stroke to be played. If this frame of mind is cultivated, as it can be, all those things which are apt to occur, even in a championship game—the lighting of a match, the flourishing of a paper, a loud remark, somebody coming in late or leaving at the wrong moment and banging his seat, etc.—will fail to disturb the player who concentrates.

Confidence

Confidence springs from knowledge of one's powers. When a player has reached the stage of excellence in performance, that knowledge of having successfully done what one has to do again is a fortifying factor beyond measure. The experienced player knows that, in spite of proved ability, periods occur when things go wrong, and he cannot do himself justice. Most players succumb then to dejection and lose faith and confidence in themselves. The wise player, however, will console himself by the knowledge that such a thing occurs to every player, even the greatest. He knows that such a period will pass, and that he has only to accept stoically its consequences, and wait patiently till "form" returns. Form is a strange thing: it comes and goes mysteriously, unaccountably, illogically. To allow its loss, which must be but temporary in a player of proved ability, to cause oneself to lose all confidence is foolish. The remedy is simply self-control and determination based on the fact of common sense that tells one: loss of form is but temporary and occasional, it happens to all, and recovery of form is certain.

Temperament

The player who allows himself to be angered or downcast by bad luck or opponents' good luck is seriously handicapping himself. Experience should tell you that, whatever the degree of bad luck you meet with, your time will come, you have proved yourself a skilled exponent of the game, and when the chances come you will take full advantage of them. So ignore all causes of irritation, etc., and, coolly and collectedly, have faith in your abilities.

Nerves

Many great players, like artists of all descriptions, are nervous. Do not try to bolster up your confidence by resorting to such weak-minded and puerile aids as "having a quick one" before the game, taking "confidence" tablets, making a great show of freedom from nerves, etc. Cultivate the feeling of wanting to "get at it", to get the chance of proving your skill, take pride in being an artist at the game, and bear in mind that the result, win or lose, comes second to pride of achievement. So long as you have shown excellence and artistry, you have succeeded, whatever the result, and people who understand the game will admire and remember you. Do all you can to win, but do not regard winning as the be-all and end-all of performance: not what you do but how you do it should be your prime purpose and pride.

PHYSICAL

Training

Billiards and Snooker demand perfect mental and physical condition as much as any game. The majority of good amateurs spend all their time (that is, the time they give to the game) in the billiard hall or club, the atmosphere of which is often stuffy, if not fetid. Most professionals look after their health, that is, they take exercise, do not smoke excessively and drink in moderation. Clark McConachy, the great New Zealand professional, actually takes a morning run in shorts every morning during the season. Joe Davis, Willie Smith and others play a lot of golf, and thus get fresh air in abundance. I recommend every serious-intentioned young amateur to attend to his health, to take regular walks, and do deep breathing and physical exercises. In this way his faculties will be fresh and his mind and body alert and attuned to action when he comes to play his important matches; and another tip, do not play or practise on the day before the big match Take it easy.

Eyesight

Look after your eyes, that is, bathe them regularly with boracic lotion, don't let the smoke get into them, and, if you do not sight the balls well at the far end of the table, see about having them tested; you may need glasses (special ones are now made for the game). Also, wear a green shade when you play. Scarcely any players do, but one I know does; he happens to be the holder of the professional world Billiards title, Clark McConachy, of New Zealand, whom I have already mentioned. A prominent amateur did, but he retired from the game not so long ago. The glare of the lights when you are low down sighting the ball can be averted by a shade.

MORAL

Lastly, *sportsmanship*! If you win, do so modestly and do not boast. Never complain, especially if losing, of the balls, the table and what not, and do not offer paltry excuses such as those we so often hear, "I've not touched a cue for days or weeks", "I haven't had time to practise", "I make dozens of 100-breaks at my club; I don't play like this", "I'm not used to these conditions", "I could give this chap 250 in 500 if I were in form" and so on. If you lose, just shake hands, congratulate your opponent and don't proffer a shred of an excuse or "explanation".

As a postscript: two valuable tips which may seem of small importance but are vitally important: (1) Stay down on the stroke, in other words, do not get up from your striking position till the stroke is complete, which often means till the balls have come to rest. Many a first-rate player misses through this fault. (2) Keep your cue chalked, and thus avoid miscueing. A mere twirl of the chalk suffices, no need to grind the tip into the chalk as many players do. Also chalk the long cues before using. Chalk on the table often causes balls to "kick" or "run off", so tap your own cue with your hand (and the long cues) after chalking, and, of course, not over the table surface. Chalk and dirt also adhere to the c-b; therefore, clean the latter occasionally, on your shirt-sleeve, not I may add on the rear portion of your anatomy, as some players do, an unsightly habit. You must not, of course, pick a ball up to clean it when it is in play (you must ask the referee to do this), but when you are in hand your opportunity occurs for cleaning the c-b, as suggested.

NOTE ON THE INDEXES

Compiling a *detailed* index of books on Billiards and Snooker has always presented a problem, owing to the mass of intricate detail involved, a single stroke, for example, often embodying a number of technical points. Hence the fact that most of the books on the subject have not included such an index. As, however, it is irritating for the reader to have to search for particular features, which the general or "contents" index cannot contain, I have included a detailed index for this book and I hope the reader will thus be able to find readily what he is in search of. It does not follow, however, that the various entries cover *every* reference in the book to the particular item; that would be impracticable; what they represent is the main treatment of such elements. The reader is reminded that many features are common to the two games and is, therefore, advised to consult both indexes.

THE AUTHOR.

BILLIARDS INDEX

SNOOKER INDEX